LIFTED OVER THE TURNSTILES
SCOTTISH FOOTBALL GROUNDS IN THE BLACK & WHITE ERA

First published in Great Britain in 2018 by DC Thomson Media. Meadowside, Dundee, Scotland DD1 9QJ
Copyright © DC Thomson & Co., Limited.
Go to www.dcthomsonshop.co.uk to purchase this book.
Or Freephone 0800 318 846. Overseas customers call +44 1382 575580
Typesetting and interior design by Steve Finan sfinan@dctmedia.co.uk

Cover design by Leon Strachan.

ISBN 978-1-8453-5719-1

Most of the photos in this book are available to buy from www.photoshopscotland.co.uk

Lifted Over The Turnstiles

Scottish Football Grounds In The Black & White Era, by Steve Finan

■ *The queue for Scotland tickets, Hampden 1959.*

■ Dens Park, 1963 – after the game.
Taking a carry-out to a football
ground was common practice.

Introduction

Football was different in the black and white days. Football grounds were different too, and how you behaved was very different.

Football holds a unique place in society, therefore the places where it is played hold a unique place in our hearts and memories. Your love affair began when you were lifted over the turnstiles as a child, it carried on into adulthood when you became addicted to the fortunes of 11 men playing in your colours.

It continued as youth turned to parenthood and a new generation joined you under the cover of those corrugated roofs. This is where your father took you, or your uncle or older sibling. This is where your memories live.

You can recall exactly where you were standing when 'that goal' went in, or 'that game' played out before you. You remember the people you were with. The halcyon days when you and your friends lived, laughed, celebrated and mourned.

The football ground is, for many, the place where you picture a now-departed loved one. This is where they took you. This is where you shared highs and lows. This is the context in which you remember them.

It is no surprise, then, that photos of the old grounds, before the passage of time and consequences of disaster changed them, are highly evocative.

I hope your home ground reaches out and talks to you.

They talk to me.

My father died, at the venerable age of 92, in 2012.

These are the places he took me as a child and they link me to him. I support the team he supported, and his father supported. It is in my blood. This is where I remember him laughing, despairing, pointing out a clever winger, telling me how and why a team's formation had changed, lifting me so I could see past the tall, great-coated and bonneted men who blocked my eight-year-old view.

In later years I travelled with my friends on scruffy special trains or ramshackle buses that trundled between Scottish cities before the modern road network made travel so much easier.

Who could fail to be moved by those journeys? The magnet of the floodlights in rain-dark skies as you marched towards the ground. There were shouts and chants in the street, the smell of food stands, the hawkers' cries and the sense of urgency and anticipation as kick-off grew near.

And afterwards, the jigs of victory or the trudge of defeat as you made your way home. Sometimes it was so crowded you could lift your feet and be carried along, wedged in the press.

Football terraces were the venues for experiences I will hold dear for all of my life. They are a part of me as they are a part of all who followed their team in the black and white era.

And that made compiling this book a joy. Unearthing old pictures became an obsession. It wasn't enough to find a good pic, the challenge was finding ones that hadn't been on every football website in every 'remember when' discussion thread.

Putting your hands on a photo that hasn't been seen for 60 years isn't easy. You can't hire a photographer to do a new set...unless you can also furnish him with a time machine.

Some of you will have seen a few of these pictures before. But there are many that lay in archive folders unloved and unseen for decades. One of the great things was that quite a few of the owners and curators were eager and proud to look out treasured shots that held their own memories.

It has been an adventure and a privilege to bring them into the light.

Steve Finan 2018

Writing a book about old stadiums became a labour of love. Football relies on nostalgia. The traditions and history of 'your' club are a huge part of what gives it character and meaning. A reverence for the home ground, and its past, is intrinsically linked.

There are many who, like me, regard old grounds as a subject of fascination. So putting this book together was a recreational pursuit. I met fellow enthusiasts and club officials up and down the country who made my quest for old photos and information a joy rather than a job of work. I was treated to many cups of tea, many biscuits and many anecdotes. I am very grateful.

A list of those I must thank is on the opposite page, but there are many more.

However, I must apologise.

I was continually frustrated that while photos of some stadiums were easy to find, others were very difficult. I fully apologise if you feel your team's ground is under-represented. This wasn't a matter of choice or bias, it was a matter of availability.

Because I know there are hundreds, probably thousands, of pictures lurking in drawers, scrapbooks or beloved collections that aren't in this book, but should be. The reason they aren't here is because I didn't know they existed. And the owners didn't know I was putting together a collection of such pictures.

But I hope, in future, we can rectify that. I hope this book will have a Volume II, if only for the selfish reason that I want to find more photos I haven't seen.

The criteria is that such photos have rarely been seen in public – or, at least, not for many years – but are deserving of wider appreciation. If you have such a photo, let's talk.

Steve Finan.

sfinan@dctmedia.co.uk

Thanks to

Gillian Martin, Jacqui Hunter, Nikki Fleming, Sylwia Jackowska, Deirdre Vincent, Craig Houston, Denise West, Barry Sullivan, David Powell, Duncan Laird, Sam Gowans, Fiona Brown, Sara Cunningham, Raymond Barr, Barry Smith, Martin Lindsay, Maggie Dun, Morris Heggie, Jeremy Bayston, Andrew Cawley, Mark Asquith, Gus Proctor, Danny Stewart, Felicity Clifford, Amy Judge, Leon Strachan, Laura Hall, John McIntosh, Fraser T. Ogilvie.

Special thanks to:

Richard McBrearty (Scottish Football Museum).

Dennis McLeary, Neil Withington and Alan Bell (Shielfield).

Duncan Carmichael (Somerset Park).

John Glencross (Recreation Park).

David Potter (Station Park).

Donnie MacBean, Andrew Ross (Victoria Park).

Allen Kyle, Scott McClymont, Christine Cuthbertson and John Livingston (Rugby Park).

Chick Young (A warm and humorous foreword).

Iain McCartney (Palmerston).

Fraser Clyne (Gayfield).

Steve Doyle (Links Park).

David Speed (Tynecastle).

Michael White (Brockville).

Jim Thomson (Annfield).

Stephen Mill (Bayview).

Ian Broadfoot (Kingsmills & Telford Street).

Tom Wright (Easter Road).

John Litster (Station Park).

Craig Brown (East End Park).

Derek Drennan (Love Street).

Robert Weir (Borough Briggs).

John Blair (Stair Park, Telford Street) – and his excellent blog: scottishfootballgroundswordpresscom. wordpress.com

■ *Shawfield in 1950. Chick (and Hotlips Hannah) are just out of shot.*

On the scoreboard:

WIN TOTAL | RACE RUNNERS | PLACE TOTAL | RACE | FORECAST

Foreword

By Chick Young

Nothing in black and white makes sense. Particularly if you're a St Mirren fan.

This is a book about the days before colour when television and photographs offered – to paraphrase Henry Ford – any colours you liked as long they were black and white.

And maybe a wee bit grey.

I'm of a certain age. I hit double figures between the rock 'n' roll years of Bill Haley's fifties and the Rubber Soul days of the Beatles and their sixties. And it was all very magical.

Good as gold me, never gave my dear old mum a minute's worry. Although she was mortified when she caught me snogging Linda Hannah at the local swing park.

Good old Hotlips Hannah, I wonder whatever became of her? She fancied me strongly, you know. Me in my shorts too. I didn't wear long trousers until I went to secondary school.

It was a golden age. I discovered friends who are still by my side today. Just can't shake them off at all.

Childhood sweethearts, endless days and summer nights playing football in the park. If practice makes perfect I should have been better than Beckham, but then enthusiasm will never replace abiliity.

And beautiful girls will never replace the beautiful game.

Football. That was the reason for living then. Still is, I suppose.

I'll never forget the first time I went into a match, young jaw dropping at the size of the crowd, the smell, the green of the grass, 22 real live players. Massage for the eyes. My own Disney World.

And, what do you know? It was all in glorious colour. And free, because the secret was to nip in for the last 20 minutes when they opened the gates to allow the departure of fans intent on early home. Or the magical 'lift over' when you begged an adult to take you in and simply lift you over the turnstile.

Impossible now of course, when turnstiles are built like prison gates.

And yet there was my mother's crazy logic when she refused to let me go to Ibrox Stadium a mile or so from home because of the size of the crowd and the consequent danger to a boy knee-high to a corner flag.

But she gave her blessing to me on alternate weeks travelling with pals to Cathkin Park, the late and lamented home of Third Lanark who died in 1967, and Shawfield Stadium, the then home of Clyde. Never mind that the latter journey involved two major bus journeys including a switch in the city centre. Can that have been safer than a stroll through the park to Ibrox?

Everything revolved around the game. Tears as well as joy. I recall listening to the radio broadcast of England against Scotland at Wembley on what was surely the newly invented transistor radio. The infancy of the invention underlined by a reception so poor

it seemed as if the commentator was saying that Scotland had lost by nine goals to three. A scoreline so ridiculous that I have never bothered checking its authenticity.

And then television.

Scotland 2, England 0 at Hampden in 1962. Goals from Davy Wilson and Eric Caldow. Black and white pictures but we knew dark blue when we saw it. Because by then I was the owner of my first V-necked Scotland strip.

There were other things in my childhood of course. Enid Blyton books, Millport and my gran's blackcurrant jam. My mother's tablet, school and the smell of freshly cut grass. And the sea. I always loved that.

But the football. Boyhood hero John White, tragically killed by lightning at his very peak. I remember him still as clearly as I recall those days of long ago.

Blessed are those whose childhood revolves around the beautiful game.

Trust me. An old football ground never lets you down. They should take Somerset Park and turn it into a museum of how grounds used to be – and in Ayr's case still is – and show generations used to the deep pile carpet and prawn sandwich approach of football's way of life in this country the days when supporters were treated like sardines.

'Preserve your memories, they're all that's left you,' wrote Paul Simon.

For those who remember the good old, bad old days, this book will help you on your way. If you're of a different, more modern time, pay attention and learn.

Scottish Football Grounds In The Black & White Era

Contents

Annfield

Stirling Albion

Adolf Hitler was instrumental in the creation of Stirling Albion.

The town of Stirling's first league team was King's Park, who played at a stadium called Forthbank. King's, formed in 1875, were never a giant of the game but can count the fathers of future Scotland boss Craig Brown and commentator Archie Macpherson as former players.

Between the wars Forthbank was, legend has it, one of the stadiums that didn't just try hosting dog racing to raise extra funds, but also cheetah racing. This wasn't a runaway success, as the cheetahs tended to not bother pursuing anything that clearly wasn't a live antelope.

On the night of April 7, 1941, a lone Luftwaffe plane dropped a bomb on Stirling. Forthbank took the hit.

King's Park played a few more friendlies, but with a ruined ground and after the long wartime hiatus they never really got going again. In their place, Stirling Albion were founded in 1945.

A group of businessmen bought the old Annfield Estate, cleared the trees and created a football ground. A stand was built the next year, and terraces laid out. The stand was rebuilt in 1949 and a West Stand put up in the early '50s.

But Albion hit hard times and sold Annfield to Stirling Council in 1981 for £250,000, then rented it back at £3,000 a year. However, the council decided their new facility should be accessible to the wider community, so Scotland's first synthetic pitch was laid in 1987 at a cost of £450,000.

By the 1990s the council were finding Annfied's running costs a burden, so built a new stadium. The club moved to the new Forthbank – not the one the Nazi bomber had taken offence to – at the end of the 1992-93 season.

Annfield existed for 48 years. It is now a housing estate.

■ *Left: Annfield in 1962.*

■ *Right: September 5, 1987 – The first game in Scottish football history that wasn't on grass (or ash, sand, snow, ice, cinders, blaes, shale, clay, cobbles, etc) saw Albion's Brian Kemp score the first ever plastic-surfaced goal.*

The Sunday Post, September 6, 1987, By Doug Baillie

STIRLING ALBION 1, AYR UNITED 1.

HAVING missed out on the Battle of Bannockburn, there's no way I'd allow another great historic event a couple of miles up the road to pass me by.

Robert Bruce was forced into doing the business on grass (kick-off 1344). Albion and Ayr found themselves locked in battle (kick-off 1500) in the first-ever senior league game on plastic turf.

Drama every square yard? A fitting match for such an occasion? Not quite, but I'll say this for the players, none looked put out on a surface which wouldn't have looked out of place in my living-room.

I confess, however, I did expect several whiffs of burning rubber when George Peebles' People and Ally MacLeod's Marauders screeched to a halt or attempted to change direction.

That didn't happen and nobody was damaged in the slightest. The sliding tackle was out, though.

Hardly surprising. No defender, I suspect, wanted to leave half a pound of his flesh on the rug.

But nothing has changed off the park. Ally MacLeod was out of his dug-out twice first-half expressing his disgust at a missed penalty by Tommy Walker, and a goal he appeared to think was not offside.

Afterwards, Ally expressed his liking for the surface. "The only problem my players had was getting their foot under the ball to cross it and get in shots. Had we been able to do that, we would have won 10-0!"

The ones which did go in looked rather sweetly stuck. Brian Kemp got the first with a "pile" driver which skidded into the corner of the net. Wee Henry Templeton (well named for playing on a carpet) hit the equaliser after weaving past a few defenders.

There were three bookings, Spence was carpeted for treating the aforementioned Henry like a doormat, McIntyre for attempting to hoover the pitch with Kemp, and Cowell for doing his duster at the referee.

Final reflections – the way things are going they'll soon be demanding plastic money at the turnstiles!

Fife Free Press, April 30, 1921

THINGS LOOK UP AT METHIL

East Fife have embarked upon a scheme of extension, which aims at providing accommodation at Bayview Park for 35,000 spectators.

Things certainly have looked up with the Methil Club ever since they won the Qualifying Cup, and there is little doubt that to improve the enclosure will prove a sound financial speculation.

A feu of the ground has been secured, which guarantees fixity of tenure.

The pitch will be carried westwards, and levelled, and the fact that the work is being undertaken just now ensures fine growth and firm turf.

A cinder track will enclose the new pitch, and a new grandstand to seat 3000 spectators is to be erected.

Bayview

East Fife

East Fife were formed in 1903 after a public meeting calling for the establishment of a senior football team in the Levenmouth area.

Because the Scottish League refused to restart the Second Division that existed before 1914, East Fife found themselves in the Central League after World War 1. The SFL imposed a wage cap on players but with the economy thriving in mining areas, and good crowds attending games, clubs like East Fife could pay better wages than national league teams and they tempted players to desert the Scottish set-up.

In 1921 the League decided it would, after all, revive its Second Division.

And the Fifers grabbed their opportunity with both hands. They were Scottish Cup finalists in 1927 and winners (while in the Second Division) in 1938. They won the League Cup three times in seven seasons in the late '40s and early '50s.

The stand was built in 1922 and seated 1,000, although the original plans had been much more ambitious (see left).

East Fife moved out of the town centre to New Bayview in 1998.

■ *Left: A snowbound Bayview in 1956.*
Right: the ground in 1970.

Boghead

Dumbarton

By the time Boghead Park closed in 2000 it was the oldest stadium in Scotland that had been in continuous use.

The club had been formed in 1872 and took up residence in 1879. The pitch was rotated 90 degrees in 1913, when the famous 'Postage Box' stand was built. It was a cosy affair with just 80 seats.

The club bought the former platform roof from Turnberry Railway Station for use as a terracing cover in 1957.

But Boghead fell further and further into disrepair as the decades passed, with Dumbarton unwilling to invest in it as they were eyeing a move to a new purpose-built facility.

This neglect had an unexpected side-effect.

Hollywood A-lister Robert Duvall, while location scouting for his regrettable 'underdog' movie *A Shot At Glory,* released in 2000, was attracted to Boghead because of its dilapidated state.

The star wanted a ramshackle ground to play the part of a 'home' for his fictitious Highland League club Kilnockie FC who, in the film, make it to the Scottish Cup Final. Bizarrely, the production company made some improvements to the stand while getting it ready for the cameras.

■ *Boghead, complete with Postage Box, in 1951.*

Borough Briggs

Elgin City

In 1938, British intelligence noticed that the Graf Zeppelin airship was sneakily taking photos of Scotland's east coast. After Norway was overrun at the start of the war, they surmised the Nazis might invade from their Scandinavian base. So a system of defensive installations was hastily constructed, stretching from the Forth estuary to Wick.

Concrete tank traps and pill boxes were built at coastal landing areas and strategic points inland, crossroads, major road and rail junctions…and Elgin City's Borough Briggs football ground.

The pill box survived until 2000 before being demolished, to the dismay of young supporters who perched on it during games.

Elgin City are the third club to bear the name, the others being short-lived teams in the 19th Century. The current club were established in 1893 and moved in to Borough Briggs in 1921.

Elgin bore the distinction of progressing further in the Scottish Cup than any other Highland League club, reaching the quarter-finals in 1968. Arguably, greater progression came in 2000 when they became the most northerly club in the Scottish (and therefore UK) league system, even if the consequent ground upgrade meant the end of the pill box.

■ *Don't panic! The pill box had slit windows all round, as those cunning Nazis might have advanced upon Borough Briggs from any direction.*

© *Robert Weir*

■ *The main stand in 1979.*

Brockville

Falkirk

Brockville was a compact, traditional Scottish football ground that was home to The Bairns from their formation in 1876 – apart from a few brief flirtations with pitches at Randyford and Blinkbonny in the 1880s – until the club moved on in 2003.

The main stand was built in 1928 and the other three sides were terracing.

The Watson Street side, opposite the main stand, gained a roof in the 1950s, though the steel beams holding up the terrace roof were low enough above the back steps to be a constant danger to taller supporters.

The ground was, however, cited as a good example of a 'safe' stadium in a 1972 report to the Government on why so many people were being injured at British football grounds. The sturdy crush barriers and concreted terracing were particularly praised.

Most football grounds of the time had ash or earthworks terraces with steps of wood dug in.

■ *The very safe (apart from the danger of head knocks) Watson Street side of Brockville.*

In 1953, Brockville was the scene for the first ever televised floodlit football match when Falkirk played host to Newcastle in a friendly.

The stadium's record attendance was 23,100, against Celtic, in the same year.

Brockville was also once the home of the world's most expensive footballer.

Falkirk had a young Englishman named Syd Puddefoot in their ranks for a few weeks when he was stationed at Bridge of Allan during the First World War. They were impressed by the centre-forward's goalscoring prowess.

Four years later, on February 7, 1922, the club paid West Ham £5,000 for Syd. The fee smashed the £4,500 Sheffield United had paid Hull City for inside-right David Mercer two years previously. This is the only occasion upon which a Scottish team has broken the world transfer fee record.

Falkirk sold Syd (for £4,000) to Blackburn Rovers three years later after he had scored 45 goals in 115 games.

■ *Brockville's 1928-built wooden stand. You can almost hear the drumming of feet and echoing calls.*

© *Historic Environment Scotland.*

■ *Broomfield in November 1950.*

Broomfield

Airdrieonians

Airdrieonians were formed in 1878 and moved in to Broomfield Park in 1892.

The famous standalone pavilion was built in 1907 and The Diamonds' capture of the 1924 Scottish Cup paid for the main stand.

The Enclosure, on the other side of the pitch gained a roof in 1959.

Broomfield was never a comfortable visit. The narrow pitch (just 67 yards), closed-in feel helped by its setting in a natural amphitheatre, and the enthusiasm of the crowd made it a feared away fixture. The tender attentions of the boys in Section B, especially from the seventies onward, made it uncomfortable for visiting fans, too.

The world's first penalty kick was awarded to Royal Albert (now a Junior team) against Airdrieonians, although at nearby Mavisbank Park in the Airdrie Charity Cup on June 6, 1891, only four days after the International Football Association Board had met in Glasgow to decide on the new rule.

Irishman James McLuggage scored, but not from 'the spot' as penalty spots hadn't yet been invented. The kick could be taken from any point on a line 12 yards from goal, and the keeper could come up to six yards forwards to narrow the angle.

Confused by all this, Airdrie lost 2-0.

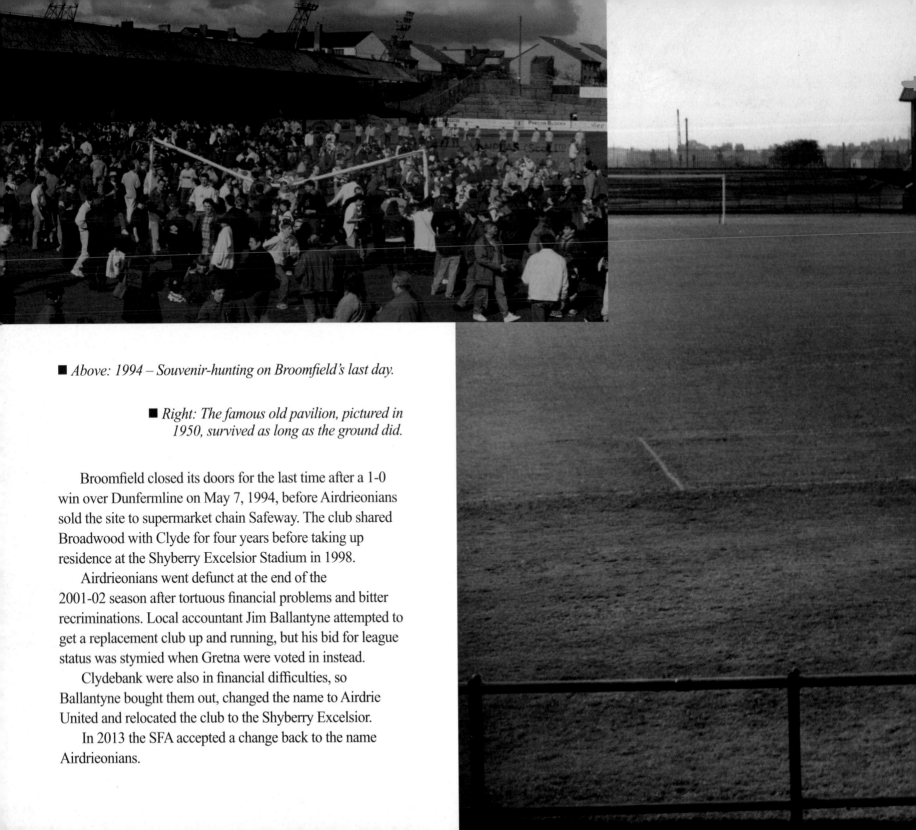

■ *Above: 1994 – Souvenir-hunting on Broomfield's last day.*

■ *Right: The famous old pavilion, pictured in 1950, survived as long as the ground did.*

Broomfield closed its doors for the last time after a 1-0 win over Dunfermline on May 7, 1994, before Airdrieonians sold the site to supermarket chain Safeway. The club shared Broadwood with Clyde for four years before taking up residence at the Shyberry Excelsior Stadium in 1998.

Airdrieonians went defunct at the end of the 2001-02 season after tortuous financial problems and bitter recriminations. Local accountant Jim Ballantyne attempted to get a replacement club up and running, but his bid for league status was stymied when Gretna were voted in instead.

Clydebank were also in financial difficulties, so Ballantyne bought them out, changed the name to Airdrie United and relocated the club to the Shyberry Excelsior.

In 2013 the SFA accepted a change back to the name Airdrieonians.

Cappielow

Morton

Morton were formed in 1874 and a degree of mystery surrounds how they got their name. The best suggestion is that inspiration came from Morton Terrace, a row of houses close to the team's original pitch.

The ground that became Cappielow had been used for several different sports before the football club took up residence in 1879. The origins of that name are shrouded too, although it is thought to be of Scandinavian origin.

The main stand was built in 1931, while the terrace opposite was roofed in 1958. The west terracing, known as the Wee Dublin End because Irish immigrants were housed behind it, was given a cover in 1978.

Morton, as they were until adding Greenock in 1994, hold the record for most promotions to and relegations from Scotland's top flight. They have been up and down 10 times and have 10 league titles despite never winning the top league. They were, however, runners-up to Celtic in 1916-17.

During the Second World War, when footballers in the forces moved to wherever they were posted, England internationals Sir Stanley Matthews and Tommy Lawton starred at Cappielow.

For a time, Morton jointly held the British midweek attendance record for the 133,750 that saw them lose a Scottish Cup Final replay 1-0 to Rangers at Hampden on Wednesday, April 21, 1948.

■ *Morton players being cheered off the Cappielow pitch after winning the Second Division title in 1964.*

■ *Morton entertain Dundee at a packed Cappielow in the early 1960s.*

Cathkin Park

Third Lanark

The story of Cathkin Park and Third Lanark, who went from a third-place finish in the old First Division to oblivion inside six years, is one of the saddest in Scottish football history.

Third Lanark Athletic Club were formed in 1872 by members of the Third Lanarkshire Rifle Volunteers.

Between 1872 and 1903 the team played at the original Cathkin Park, in the Crosshill area of Glasgow, that the regiment had used as a drill ground.

They moved in to a new ground when Queen's Park left after being refused permission to extend it to allow for larger crowds. QP had called it Hampden, but Thirds named it New Cathkin Park.

Thirds were to play at New Cathkin Park until being liquidated in 1967.

The Hi-Hi's last game was a 3-3 draw with Queen of the South on Tuesday, April 25. The previous home game, on Saturday, April 15 (the same day Scotland beat England 3-2 at Wembley) had drawn their lowest ever crowd. Just 297 watched them beat Clydebank 1-0.

■ *Right: the barrel-roofed old main stand being demolished in 1962, to make way for an updated version. The new one would be used for less than five years.*

There was many a false dawn before the sun finally set on Thirds.

As the 1966-67 season came to an end, the club's board said they would sell Cathkin Park for housing and create a new stadium in Bishopbriggs. But it never happened.

The final blow was a petition over a £2,000 bill from a building company who had worked on the grandstand several years previously. A winding up order was issued at the Court of Session on June 7, 1967.

The new grandstand had been completed in 1963, but after the demise of the club it became a vandalised shell. For decades the stadium, with its old-fashioned pavilion still in the corner, grew ever more forlorn.

The terraces still exist, although much reduced in size from the ground's hey-day. But the pitch, used as an overflow car park for Hampden in the 1970s and '80s, has been re-laid and is now used for amateur games.

Cathkin Park, one of the nation's great old stadiums where nine Scottish Cup Finals were played, now exists mostly as a memory.

■ *1968. After being abandoned, the 'new' stand and the pavilion quickly fell prey to vandals.*

Celtic Park

Celtic

■ *The frontage of Celtic Park on a damp day in 1962.*

Celtic were formed in 1888 and for the first four years of their existence played on a field a stone's throw from the current Celtic Park on the north east corner of what is now Springfield Road (it was Dalmarnock Street in those days) and London Road.

A team of volunteers had levelled a pitch, with an earth bank serving as terracing around three sides and an open-to-the-skies grandstand containing dressing rooms, toilets and an office.

This land was leased, however, and when the rent was raised from £50 to a usurious £450 per year, the club relocated a few hundred yards west to the site of a former brickyard. An army of volunteers again turned out to create a second Celtic Park in time for the 1892-93 season.

A structure intended solely for journalists was built in 1894, the first 'press box' ever created in any football ground in the world.

■ *Left: Another view of the main entrance, from the railway line that used to run alongside.*

■ *Right: Around 60,000 supporters welcomed Celtic home with the European Cup in 1967.*

■ *September 1950. An expectant crowd at a full Celtic Park, just before the teams emerge.*

Legions of Celtic supporters know their ground as 'Paradise'.

The origins of the name, however, aren't agreed upon. One version has it that a supporter looking at the stadium next to the huge Eastern Necropolis commented: 'It's like moving from the graveyard to Paradise', and the name took root from there.

Another, possibly more accountable, version is that the name was inspired by a speech made by club chairman John H. McLaughlin at an early AGM. It was said that: 'A desert would become a Garden of Eden', referring to the move to the new ground in 1892 and its transformation by many willing hands.

This, in turn, inspired another club member to eloquence, saying the players might: 'Dream of Paradise when flitting on its sward.'

Celtic FC became very popular almost instantly after formation. With crowds being attracted in the tens of thousands a double-deck stand, the first in Britain, was constructed on the Janefield Street side of the playing area.

It burned down in 1904 and was replaced by a curved-roof covered terracing that became known as 'The Hayshed'.

In 1927 the main stand also suffered a fire and was replaced, two years later, by a new grandstand designed by Archibald Leitch.

In 1957 the Celtic End had a partial roof built over the terracing and the opposite end was given a new roof in the late 1960s.

The Hayshed (by then known as 'The Jungle') was given a new roof in 1966.

The main stand was rebuilt with a cantilevered roof in 1971.

■ *Left: An aerial shot of Celtic Park in 1963.*

■ *Right: Apprentice Tommy Henderson gets in a bit of stamina training with a wheelbarrow in 1959.*

■ *The West End was refurbished in 1967 with a new roof to the same design as the one over Hampden's West End. This gave the Celtic Park of the time more covered terracing than any British ground, apart from Wembley. This picture was taken in the close-season of 1967*

■ *Left: A 1958 view of Celtic Park, Janefield Cemetery and The Parkhead Forge. Top right is Carntyne dog track.*

■ *Right: The Jungle got a fence in 1975.*

Central Park

Cowdenbeath

Central Park, as the name suggests, is close to the centre of the Fife town and has been home to The Blue Brazil since 1917.

The club is the oldest in Fife, being formed in 1881, or 1882. The uncertainty over a precise date is down to the intricacies of the various amalgamations of former miners' teams that culminated in the formation of Cowdenbeath FC. Some were said to have played games after the date when they were thought to have merged.

Central Park's Main Stand was built in 1921. Half of it was destroyed in a fire in 1992.

Greyhound racing started in 1928. Stock car racing crashed into the stadium in 1970 and has remained parked there ever since.

Central Park is in one of Scotland's great mining areas. The Cowdenbeath No.7 Coal Mine, which opened in 1869 and closed in 1960 after providing exacting and difficult employment for generations of hard Fife men, was immediately behind the main stand. A park and leisure centre now stand on the site.

■ *Fife's mining villages have a reputation for being tough. Indeed, there's not much a Fife miner can't cope with...but even they couldn't play on this monsoon-hit pitch in 1970. The game was postponed.*

The Big Build Up

Football grounds evolved. The idea of a large arena with stands and terracing didn't exist before about 1890. Football was a pastime, not a business. There was no need to cater for tens of thousands of spectators. Then, suddenly, there was. Football became incredibly popular and every town and city had a team.

These football grounds grew into major landmarks, though the amount of planning into where they were placed was minimal. Some were close to the rail network, some were surrounded by tenements, some were on weather-blasted heaths.

The clubs collected earth, rubble, ash and rubbish to form into banks, which had wooden slats or old railway sleepers to make steps and these eventually became terraces. They had pavilions where the players changed and which sometimes had seats to give a view of the pitch. Then they had grandstands so people could watch in comfort. Then some put up roofs over the terraces to hold off the worst of the wind and rain.

Some became giants built for 150,000, others were more modest. Each was built in accordance with the amount of money available, or the idiosyncrasies of their space and terrain, or the ambitions of the officials ordering their construction.

Some changed slowly, some saw huge projects that swiftly altered the look and feel of the ground. Most were remodelled on several subsequent occasions.

Every one was unique. There was no prefabricated or one-design-fits-all approach. Each ground had its quirks, flaws, advantages and drawbacks.

Each had to undergo some sort of construction process.

■ *Left and right: Ibrox has seen many changes over the years.*
See also Ibrox on Page 134.

New Kilbowie got a new stand in 1967, to complement the enclosure in front of and below the social club, which opened in 1966.

Membership fees were five bob (25p) a week.

There were worries from patrons (and some players) that the large windows of the club wouldn't stand up to the rigours of a size 5 hoofed from the pitch. However, the management gave assurances that the very latest bullet-proof (and therefore hopefully also proof against a leather 'tub' on a wet day) glass had been used.

It was all part of Clydebank's rise under the Steedman brothers. The Saturday before this picture was taken in September 1967, The Bankies had drawn a crowd of 6,000 to their League Cup play-off with Ayr United.

The club were on the up. Clydebank would, within a few years, find and sign a genuine superstar in Davie Cooper. They made it to the Premier League in 1977.

See also New Kilbowie on Page 160.

■ *The new stand and social club in 1967.*

■ *Dundee United were the first club in Scotland to have a cantilevered stand, with no supporting pillars encroaching on the view. Sheffield Wednesday and Scuthorpe were the only English clubs to have such stands, but United's was the first, in 1961, to attempt to bend round a corner. It required the complete removal of the old stand (left) before the new steel frame could be constructed (right). In those days, when Health & Safety rules were a little more relaxed, the new stand was used before it was entirely finished...or had things regarded as necessities in the namby-pamby modern era, like stairs to climb up to it. See also Tannadice on Page 224.*

Station Park, overlooking the Vale of Strathmore, sees a lot of weather. The roof of the first grandstand, which faces the prevailing wind, was blown off by a gale before it had even been officially opened in 1888, and torn off again in an 1893 storm. Another windstorm, on the night of February 4-5, 1957, ripped the stand apart again.

Robust measures were required, and the Forfar support rose to the occasion. The club, led by the money and manpower controlled by chairman William Callander, started a fundraising campaign.

One of the great Scottish sides of the era, Hearts, brought their first team to Station Park for a friendly to help the cash drive. The Edinburgh men refused to take any share of the 3,000 gate and, thanks to those generous actions, to this day older Forfar supporters retain a soft spot for the Tynecastle club.

Forfar were drawn against Rangers in the 1958 Scottish Cup and running repairs were made to the old stand in time for the first ever meeting of the clubs in official competition. It was, sadly for The Loons, a 1-9 loss but the gate receipts were very welcome.

Once enough money had been raised to begin a new stand, one with columns to hold up the roof – and also keep it securely bolted down – work got under way. Much of the labour was done by volunteers. This went well over the summer, the new stand being constructed close behind the old one.

When the weather turned, work stopped for the winter.

But fate was about to take a hand.

■ *The aftermath of the 1957 storm. If ever a grandstand needed rebuilding....*

Forfar drew Rangers at home in the cup again only a season after the last tie. You wait 70 years for a Rangers game, then two come along at once!

Forfar had six weeks to get the new stand complete.

The volunteers ignored the cold weather and redoubled their efforts, working long and hard, Sabbath days included, to get the ground ready for January 31, 1959.

They made it by the skin of their teeth and the club awarded the hard-grafting volunteers with stand tickets for the Rangers game. They were further rewarded by a much improved display on the pitch, the home side losing only 3-1 this time.

Their craftmanship is a testament to them. The new stand is still in place today, 60 years later – and after many a blowy Angus day in the years between.

See also Station Park on Page 220.

See also Station Park on Page 220.

■ *Left: Volunteers working on the new Station Park stand.*

■ *Right: The new stand... and the old stand.*

Cliftonhill

Albion Rovers

Albion Rovers were founded in 1882, an amalgamation of two Coatbridge clubs Albion FC and Rovers FC. They have played at Cliftonhill, Coatbridge, since Christmas Day 1919.

Their previous home was at Meadow Park in Whifflet, now a suburb of Coatbridge but once a mining village close to the town.

Football in Scotland's lower reaches was sporadic for much of World War 1, so the last game Rovers had played at Meadow Park had been on March 6, 1915.

The plan was to take the existing pavilion from Meadow Park to the new ground at Cliftonhill and be ready for the start of the 1919-1920 season.

But the work to get the new stadium ready took longer than expected and Rovers had to play home games at local rival Airdrie's Broomfield Park until late December.

The uncertainty and ground-hopping didn't help Rovers' league form, they finished bottom of Division One. But they did manage to reach the Scottish Cup final for the first, and so far only, time in the club's history. Sadly, they were edged out 3-2 by Kilmarnock.

■ *Cliftonhill's wide open spaces in 1951.*

■ *Above: Cliftonhill has been no stranger to big crowds over the years.*

■ *Right: 1951 – The vast bowl of Cliftonhill is an excellent setting for a football gound.*

The ground has, like many in Scotland, hosted dog racing and speedway in an effort to raise extra revenue.

Cliftonhill's open aspect had long been eyed as a speedway venue, but while the overall acreage was vast, the bowl-like area around the pitch wasn't considered quite big enough.

It took the innovative (for speedway) and somewhat detrimental (for football) decision to run the racetrack up the terracing at either end, creating a highly unusual banked track, to solve the problem.

Dens Park

Dundee

Dundee and Dundee United famously have grounds less than 200 yards from each other. The only clubs in Europe with closer stadiums are MTK, Hungary's most successful club, and third division BKV Elore in Budapest, whose grounds are directly across the street from each other.

There has been an enduring myth in the city of Dundee that the main stand at Dens was a cast-off from Ibrox. This isn't true. The stand at Dens was designed by Archibald Leitch, the same architect who created Ibrox, but the link ends there.

The kinked main stand, on the Tannadice Street/Sandeman Street side of Dens, opened in 1921 as a replacement for a previous and smaller stand, whereas Ibrox underwent major improvements in 1899 and 1928. To clinch the argument, there wasn't a second-hand grandstand available from Ibrox within the timeframe.

■ *Left: Dens Park, with Tannadice in the background, in 1955.*

■ *'The Derry', home of Dundee's loudest young fans, got bench seats in 1980.*

Dundee Courier, December 21, 1899

DUNDEE FOOTBALL CLUB BAZAAR

In some respects the Football Club Bazaar has fallen on an unfortunate season, for between the wretched weather, the near approach of Christmas, and the general depression regarding the war, folks have neither much money nor inclination for such functions.

However, if there is one object which appeals to the many, and which is calculated to procure hard cash at the most unpropitious of times, it the great and glorious game of football.

There is little doubt that the footballers of Dundee will to a man rally round the Dundee Club, which has so pluckily undertaken all the difficulties and responsibilities incidental to the getting of a big bazaar.

The sum aimed at is £1500, which it is hoped will be sufficient to settle the team free of debt in their new quarters at Dens Park.

The Kinnaird Hall, which has worn in its time so many varied dresses, is this week clothed in atmosphere of ancient splendour. The scheme of decoration, carried out by Wilkinson & Company, Liverpool, is the representation of well-known castles and abbeys. Quaint arches and turrets constitute the surroundings to the stalls, and round the entire gallery hang large pieces of scenery, showing Melrose Abbey, Balmoral Castle, Loch Leven, &c. The effect is simple but striking, and the goods show well against the sombre background.

The Dundee Club Stall articles range from a doll to a donkey, the latter being a good specimen of the usual four-legged variety. A China dinner service there is too, a marble clock, a very handsome double wardrobe, and an Eagle bicycle, a silver service, a dressing case, and a couple life-sized baby dolls.

I noticed, too, several pretty opals, a few good flower pots, and a multitude of the smaller bazaar articles.

■ *Above, early fundraising efforts. Right – Fans arrive at Dens by tram and car in 1947.*

■ *Dens Park in 1952, before the roof was put on the south terracing.*

Dundee FC were formed in 1893 and played at Carolina Port in their early years. They moved in to Dens Park in 1899 and bought the land outright in 1919 for £5,000.

The transfers of Davie Sneddon and celebrated goalie Bill Brown, to Preston and Tottenham respectively, in 1959, for a combined total of £29,500, paid for the south terracing cover and installation of floodlights.

The south side is known locally as 'The Derry', although the reason why is often disputed.

The Provost Road end was covered in the mid-1960s, although the roof didn't stretch the entire width of the pitch.

The most glorious year of the club's existence, so far, was the league championship of season 1961-62.

■ *Left: A 1950s crowd packs the enclosure beneath the main stand and the T. C. Keay end, named for the engineering firm that displayed its name on its roof there for several decades.*

■ *Right: Roofing The Derry and putting up floodlights in 1959.*

DUNDEE "SKATE" TO TOP
THEY HAD RANGERS ON THE RUN

Dundee 3, Rangers 1.

On an ice rink surface at Dens Park yesterday Dundee brought off a double-barrelled victory over Rangers.

They avenged their League Cup semi-final defeat and displaced the Ibrox team from the top of the league.

Dundee are now in a splendid position to go ahead and make history by winning the championship flag.

Johnny Pattillo

Quick-Fire Goals.

Disputed Goal Rattled Fifers

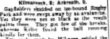

Number Two.

Superb Save.

TWO HAT-TRICKS V. ARBROATH

■ *Above: A report of the Dundee v. Rangers League Cup tie on January 4, 1949, and, right, the crowd queuing to get in to that game, with at least two sneak-ins over the wall. Most grounds had a few weak spots that could be used to bypass the turnstiles...if no one was looking.*

Douglas Park

Hamilton Academical

Accies were formed in 1874 by the rector and pupils of Hamilton Academy. Their early homes were at Bent Farm, South Avenue and South Haugh, before the move to Douglas Park in 1888.

In 1913 they opened a main stand, designed by Archibald Leitch. It was 90 yards long with a curved wooden roof and seated 1,221. A stand was also built on the other side of the pitch after World War 1, but lasted only five years before being destroyed by a fire. It became terracing, which got a roof in 1949.

Accies fans got a fright in 1970 when the club briefly ceased to exist. They had finished bottom of the Second Division and, riddled with debt, resigned from the league. After missing the first two games of the 1970-71 season, a group of directors stepped in to save the day.

■ *Pre-season training, in modern days of electronic monitoring, sports science, and fitness centres, has come a long way. But players of the black & white era weren't allowed to slack. Trainers dreamed up all sorts of diabolical ways to get their charges to sweat, including employing any parts of the stadium that looked useful. Few clubs had training pitches, far less a complex, elsewhere. Vaulting the perimeter fence – as these Accies players are displaying at Douglas Park – along with sprints up the terracing steps, were favourite instruments of torture. And with less protection from referees, wrestling was, obviously, a useful skill.*

The Douglas Park pitch had one of the bigger slopes in Scottish football, a nine-foot difference end-to-end. It was also one of the last grounds to get floodlights, which finally arrived in 1971.

Talk of a new stadium began as far back as the '80s, but took years to reach a conclusion, with Douglas Park falling into an ever more dilapidated state. By 1993 the main stand had been declared unsafe and the capacity of the remaining terracing was restricted to 4,000.

Accies moved out at the end of the 1993-94 season, but didn't have a new home, so spent seven seasons as tenants at Cliftonhill and Firhill. They sold Douglas Park to a supermarket chain and eventually moved into New Douglas Park next door. The turnstiles were sold to Falkirk and part of the main stand went to Juniors powerhouse Auchinleck Talbot for £30,000.

Accies kept their floodlights, though, to put up at the new ground.

■ *The wooden-roofed stand at the old Douglas Park was a rare long-surviving example of the architectural term 'a Belfast Truss Roof'. This design, made of timber and characterised by a barrel-shaped roof, was commonly used in industrial buildings, aircraft hangars and terracing covers (including at Celtic Park and Ibrox) between the mid-1860s and World War 1, after which steel-girder roofs with straight lines took over.*

© Dunfermline Athletic FC

East End Park

Dunfermline Athletic

Dunfermline Athletic sprang to life in 1885 after a dispute over membership resulted in a split from Dunfermline Football Club, which in turn had been formed as a winter sports section of Dunfermline Cricket Club.

Athletic initially existed as an amateur outfit until 1899. The new body had taken up residence at East End Park, securing a lease on ground owned by the North British Railway Company.

They entered the Scottish Football League Division Two in 1912, a relatively late date, and quite surprising as East End Park was recording attendances as high as any club outside Glasgow and Edinburgh in the first decade of the 20th Century.

■ *Left and right: East End Park in the 1960s.*

Funded by The Pars' glorious Scottish Cup win of 1961, a modern stand was constructed on the Halbeath Road side in 1962.

In the '30s, income from greyhound racing at East End Park all but saved the club, but the track curving over the playing surface made the taking of corners a slightly difficult proposition.

In 1965 the North Terrace roof was extended to cover the town end to form an L-shaped "shed".

East End Park also holds a curious place in British maritime history. Wood from RMS Mauretania, once the most celebrated ship in the British merchant fleet, was used to improve the east terracing in 1935.

The Mauretania was the world's biggest ship when launched in 1906 and held the Blue Riband for the fastest transatlantic crossing from 1909 to 1929. The great ship was being broken up at Rosyth Dockyard when The Pars salvaged some of her timber and laid it for Fifers to stand on.

■ *The Pars have a tradition of being a well-supported club. Pictured right is the final day of the 1967-68 season.* See also Crowd Scenes, Pages 168-177.

■ Crowds gather for the first Edinburgh derby of the 1954-55 season.

Easter Road

Hibernian

Easter Road Stadium is named for its location in the area of the eastern thoroughfare to Leith from Edinburgh. Maps from the 18th Century show a counterpart, Wester Road (now Broughton Road and Bonnington Road), taking traffic from Edinburgh old town north to the great Forth port.

Hibs, formed in 1875, led a nomadic existence like most football teams of the time before the sport became big enough business to merit the invention of enclosed stadiums.

And Hibs, despite shaky beginnings, became big business. Their first more-or-less permanent home was Hibernian Park, also in the Easter Road area, midway between the club's two bases of support, Little Ireland in the Cowgate and the Catholic population of Leith.

It was at Hibernian Park, known to supporters as The Holy Ground, that Hibs became Association Football Champions of the World, by defeating England's 'Invincibles' Preston North End on August 13, 1887.

The title of 'world champions' was, largely, applied to the game retrospectively, and somewhat ambitiously. But the defeat of a side about to achieve the first ever 'double' in English football, completing the league season unbeaten, should not be underestimated.

■ *Easter Road in 1971.*

■ *The two-tiered terracing on the East Side.*

The move to Easter Road came in 1890 when the lease for Hibernian Park expired. The club had nowhere to go. For a year, all fixtures were played away from home. All bar one. The team played a 'home' game at Leith Athletic's Hawkhill in 1891. But permanent terms couldn't be reached.

It was a difficult time and Hibs temporarily ceased to exist in late 1891 before being revived in 1892.

The committee secured a lease on a field at Drum Park and, after frantic work to create a viable ground, the new Easter Road hosted its first game, a challenge match against Clyde on February 4, 1893.

The resurrected club went from strength to strength. Easter Road wasn't an ideal site, it had a slope and was difficult to get to, but a stand with dressing rooms was built and terraces were erected round the other three sides of the pitch.

It took several years for long-term security to be achieved. Hibs considered several other venues around Edinburgh and even a relocation to Aberdeen before, in 1922, a 25-year lease on Easter Road was secured and an ambitious development phase began.

The playing surface was moved 40 yards east, lessening the effect of the slope. Three banks of terracing were raised and a main grandstand built on the west side with the help of £4,000 (a world record fee for a goalkeeper) from Arsenal for Bill Harper.

The capacity of the new ground was listed as 45,000.

■ *A snowy Easter Road in mid-February 1960.*

Further development raised the height of the terraces until a crowd of 65,860 saw the Edinburgh derby with Hearts on January 2, 1950.

The overcrowding to achieve this figure, the highest ever recorded at a football match in Edinburgh, had been so bad that an upper tier extension to the east terracing was put in place.

The Hibs board even drew up plans to extend the north and south terraces to match the height of the east, which would have given the ground a capacity close to 100,000.

Hibs were also pioneers of football ground floodlight pylons.

Their 100-foot steel towers in each corner of the ground, which took six weeks to be built in 1954, were the first of their kind anywhere in the world. Every other club who had lights before this had mounted them on the roofs of their existing stands or terraces.

Local engineering company Miller & Stables, who built the structures, went on to put up pylons for 'drenchlights', as they termed them, at many more grounds including Celtic Park, Tynecastle, Hampden, Tannadice, and Newcastle United's St James Park.

■ *Easter Road's drenchlighting on pylons was the wonder of world football.*

The Easter Road slope was famous in Scottish football for more than 100 years.

Until the pitch was levelled at the end of the 1999-2000 season, the playing surface was six feet three inches higher at the Dunbar End than at the North 'home' end.

It was traditional, and psychologically important, for Hibs to win the toss and choose to kick down the slope towards the North End terracing in the second half of games.

■ *The view down the slope in 1970.*

Firhill

Partick Thistle

The obvious question is: why don't Partick Thistle play in the Partick area of Glasgow? Their home ground Firhill is, of course, a few miles north in Maryhill.

The shipping industry is to blame.

Thistle were formed in 1876 and played in several places before settling at Meadowside Park on the northern bank of the inner Clyde estuary in 1891. Their record crowd there was 16,000 for a cup-tie against Hibs.

However, they didn't own the ground and with ship construction booming, the owners sold Meadowside to the shipbuilders next door, who were expanding. Thistle had to move, and move quick.

Thistle fairly rapidly secured land in Maryhill, making a £5,500 purchase from the Caledonian Railway company (that cheque is still on show at Firhill).

■ *Firhill in 1976 – it used to be said that the best view of the pitch was from the surrounding tenements.*

The new ground wasn't quite ready in time, though. Thousands turned up for a scheduled game on August 21, only to find cancelled signs on the gates because the Office Of Public Works had declared the stand wasn't yet fit for use. *The Scottish Referee*, a sports newspaper published between 1888 and 1914, called this: 'A debacle unparalleled in the history of British sport', which may have been a slight exaggeration.

Firhill wasn't used for a game until October 2, 1909, so Partick spent the 1908-09 season playing their home games anywhere and everywhere, even as far away as Aberdeen. The season didn't go well, Thistle gaining just eight points from 34 games and finishing bottom of the league.

By 1922 things were looking up and Firhill saw a 49,838 crowd for a league game with Rangers. The ground was quickly extended, the main stand being constructed in time for the 1927-28 season. Firhill's biggest ever crowd, 54,728, was recorded for a Scotland v Ireland international in 1928.

The enclosure roof was put up in the 1950s and floodlights followed in 1955, inaugurated in a friendly with Tottenham Hotspur.

■ *Firhill in 1970.*

Note the admission price above the turnstiles of 20p, or four shillings. This is an indictment of the football industry worldwide, not just of Partick Thistle. According to the Office for National Statistics Composite Price Index, the pound sterling has experienced an average inflation rate of 5.80% per year between 1970 and today. That means the spending power of 20p in 1970 equates to £3 in 2018.

What A How-Do-You-Do At Firhill!

BY JACK HARKNESS

PARTICK THISTLE v. FALKIRK. Result—Chaos. Attendance—about 4000 paid to get in; about 4500 received vouchers on the way out entitling them to get their money back.

● At one o'clock Referee Alistair McKenzie inspected Firhill. He declared the ground playable.

● At 2.15 the Firhill gates were opened and the turnstiles started clicking merrily.

The gathering crowd had plenty to keep them interested. Every Thistle reserve player and lots of willing helpers armed with brooms were gaily sweeping pools of water from the playing field.

One pool up in the south-east corner was rather deep. We had the amazing spectacle of a couple of youths actually using shovels to lift the water and shovel it into a barrow. Then a barrowload of water was wheeled to the touch-lines.

It was all very enjoyable for a short time. But things became a trifle ominous when it was noticed that no sooner had one pool been cleared of water than it started filling up again.

"Mineral Springs"

In the past we have associated Firhill with many things. But we never knew anything about underground mineral springs. Here these springs were working overtime, as the water came bubbling up all over the place.

● At 2.45 the referee called for a ball. It was kicked around for a while.

● At 2.50 he called on the two managers to join him in a serious discussion.

● At 2.53 he declared the game off.

The gates were immediately closed. An announcement was made that spectators would receive a ticket on the way out entitling them to admission when the game was played.

What followed then is just nobody's business. Hostile booing broke out all over the terracing.

Several hundred gathered at each end of the stand demanding their money back.

Police Snowballed

The police tried to do their best, but were met with a barrage of snowballs. People in adjacent houses must have thought the game was going on because of the cheering which greeted every snowball that found its target.

Another announcement told the fans the ticket they received would entitle the holders to admission to any home game at Firhill except the Rangers game, and also that, if anyone desired, they could have the cash refunded at Firhill, on production of the voucher, any day this week.

Behind the scenes, little groups of club officials were holding conferences.

● *Should one man be able to cause such a stramash in football?*

● *Should the two managers not inspect the ground, and if they decide its playable, then the game should go on —with the referee coming into things only if they disagree?*

It was a thousand pities Partick Thistle should have suddenly found themselves with this on their plates. They acted strictly in accordance with the rules.

But whether the referee should not, at one o'clock, have anticipated the weather conditions — well, that's different story.

■ *Left, February 9, 1963 – The Firhill crowd demands a refund, and The Sunday Post tells us why.*

Fir Park

Motherwell

Motherwell FC were formed in 1886 and played on several patches of green around the town before 1895, when they took over a wooded area owned by local coal baron and politician Lord Hamilton of Dalziel. His racing colours were claret and amber, so the team adopted those colours.

The east terracing was roofed in 1954, but Fir Park's predominant feature had always been the old main stand, which was extended in 1921 but still only held around 1,000 people.

This lasted through the John Hunter-inspired glory years of the '20s and '30s until 1962, when Ian St John was transferred to Liverpool. His £37,500 fee (along with the Pat Quinn transfer to Blackpool a year later) helped pay for the construction of a new main stand.

But that new stand ran into a problem.

■ *This 1950 photo shows the old main stand at Fir Park.*

The new stand's steel structure was, quite innovatively, built around the existing stand so that spectators could still use it during construction.

The main frame of the steelwork was put in place, but it was at this point that the problem arose.

The club found they couldn't come to terms with one of the adjacent house owners, who complained that the new stand would plunge their garden into eternal shadow.

With money for the project running low, and refusing to be held to ransom, the board had no choice but to alter their plans.

Rather than have the new stand run the full length of the pitch, they stopped building roughly level with the edge of the penalty box.

Eventually, agreement was reached with the home owner, but the rest of the stand was never completed. The extra piece of frame, however, remains in place to this day.

Like most other grounds, Fir Park's terraces 'grew'. They were extended, little by little, in fits and starts, with cartloads and barrowloads of earth and ash. When tall enough for another step to be built, a strip of wood was entrenched in.

The ground was eventually big enough to take crowds of 35,000-plus.

The southern end, known in its day as the Estate End (which would have the current huge two-tier stand built in the early 1990s) was terraced with concrete in 1932.

■ *The new stand project was created above and around the wooden original, keeping the new banks of seating at the same angle as the old.*

■ *Doubly dry with two roofs to guard against the North Lanarkshire rain.*

■ *The stand lost 1-0 to the house, but the space left did create a great place to hang out the team kit.*

Firs Park

East Stirlingshire

East Stirlingshire's history is a triumph of dedication and perseverance. They are no longer in the Scottish league system and no longer play at Firs Park. But it would be a foolish man who would suggest this has daunted The Shire.

The gentlemen of Bainsford Bluebonnets Cricket Club started a football team, Bainsford Britannia, in 1880. The footballers changed their name to East Stirlingshire the following year and played their home games at Bainsford village's Merchiston Park. But in 1920 construction of a railway line across the pitch forced a move and a derelict factory site a few miles away in Falkirk, at Firs Street, was selected as the new home. The club's record attendance, 12,000, was set the following year when Partick Thistle, on their way to winning the trophy, faced Shire in a Scottish Cup tie.

In a highly controversial move, Shire's board merged the club with Clydebank Juniors to form a new club, East Stirlingshire Clydebank, in 1964. The new club played at New Kilbowie Park – and took Firs Park's enclosure roof and floodlights with it, as well as their place in the league system. But a legal challenge by fans restored The Shire to existence after only one season and they returned to Firs Park.

The roof and lights never did.

■ *Firs Park in 1963, before the enclosure roof made its way west.*

The ground had its main stand replaced in 1992 with a structure that looked very like the old one.

At the end of the 2007-08 season SFA regulations were demanding substantial improvements to the ground, including lengthening the pitch which would have required digging up a good proportion of the terracing.

It wasn't cost-efficient, so Shire moved out to begin a ground-share with Stenhousemuir that was intended to last five years.

The last ever league game at Firs Park was a special one. The team had to beat Montrose to avoid finishing bottom of the Scottish Football League system for a sixth year in succession. They duly won 3-1 and were placed second bottom by one point. Glory comes in many guises.

The Shire finished bottom of Scottish League Two in 2016-17 and lost a play-off 2-1 on aggregate to Edinburgh City, so ending a 61-year stay in the Scottish national leagues.

They now play in the Lowland League and are still sharing Ochilview.

■ *The view over rooftops to the old Firs Park.*

Shire's chairman Willie Muirhead went to West Germany for the 1974 World Cup. He asked another Scottish manager, himself on the rise, if he could recommend a similar type of man to manage his club. That young gun was Ally MacLeod and the man he recommended was a 32-year-old named Alex Ferguson.

The later Sir Alex had been a player for Ally at Ayr United the previous season, scoring nine goals in 24 games. Fergie was approached to take the Shire job and agreed to cut his managerial teeth at Firs Park.

However, the future Aberdeen and Manchester United boss was in charge at Firs Park for only 117 days, before being lured away to St Mirren. Sir Alex has since said that he thoroughly enjoyed his time at Firs Park and only moved on the advice of his friend and mentor Jock Stein.

■ *Left – the main stand at Firs Park.*

■ *Right – the Firs Street entrance to the ground as it was in 1963.*

Gayfield

Arbroath

Locals say that Gayfield is a great place for fresh air. Visitors, to the derision of many a Red Lichtie, have claimed that it is cold.

There isn't a stadium in Europe that is closer to the sea than Gayfield, just a short throw-in across a road and the wall that stops the full rigours of the North Sea from invading the terracing, although particularly big waves will send spray as far as the pitch. Corner-takers on the shore side at the Queen's Drive end have been known to suffer a seawater shower if the wind is in the right quarter.

Arbroath FC were formed in 1878 (they are Scotland's oldest club north of the central belt) and played at Woodville Park and Hospitalfield before acquiring a rubbish tip at the sea front in 1880.

The present 'Greater' Gayfield Park

overlies part of the original ground. The old one was partially demolished in 1925 and the pitch moved 60 yards, the former halfway line becoming the new goal line.

More land had to be purchased to move the pitch, at a cost of £1,050, £750 of which was raised by public subscription. The old stand was taken down and reconstructed on the opposite side of the pitch. The pitch was also extended to 120 x 70 yards (it is now 115 x 71) but the extension was a necessity.

The old pitch had been very narrow, hemmed in by the road on one side and shoreline on the other. It was so tightly wedged in that there wasn't even room for supporters on the Dundee Road side. This had resulted in problems over the years.

Rangers were defeated 4-3 in a Scottish Cup tie in 1884 but complained that the pitch was too small for senior football. Their appeal was successful and the game was ordered to be played again. Arbroath lost the replay 8-1.

■ *Gayfield in October 1950, before the erection of floodlights in 1955.*

The Advertiser
September 14, 1885

BON-ACCORD 0 v. ARBROATH 36

The fixture of these clubs in the first round of the Scottish Cup ties was played off on Saturday afternoon. The ballot gave the Bon-Accord the selection of the ground, but they chose to come to Gayfield. The weather was unpleasant, and as a consequence the turn-out of spectators was not particularly large. At half-past three the teams faced each other — the maroons looking towards the west goal. The Aberdonians kicked off and almost at once the ball was in their territory. A short scrimmage sent the leather out, but on being thrown in it was sent towards the strangers' goal, and Crawford administered the finishing kick which secured the first point. This was the beginning of a one-sided game. The maroons, working in fine form, had everything their own way — the defence play of the Bon-Accord being unworthy of that name. Goal after goal was notched, and at half time the score stood Arbroath 15; Bon-Accord 0.

Things looked no brighter for the strangers in the second half, all the action being practically in the vicinity of their goal posts, and when the whistle blew time the game stood thus — Arbroath, 36; Bon Accord, 0. Forty goals in all were scored, but four were disallowed by the referee for offside. Only once during the game did the colours of the maroons seem in danger of being lowered, but Collie saved. The play of the Aberdeen team all through, as can be imagined, was most mediocre, and regards the individual work there was next to nothing worthy the least praise. The goals were taken as follows by the maroons:- Petrie 13; Munro 7; Robertson 6; Crawford 6; Marshall 2; Tackett 2. The Arbroath team were:- Milne, goal, Salmond and Collie, backs; Milne and Rennie, half-backs; Robertson, Crawford, Petrie, Marshall, Tackett, and Munro, forwards. Milne, the half-back, was captain of the team for the day.

It is believed that the score piled up by the maroons is unequalled in the annals of football.

■ *Gayfield's playing surface has been moved 60 yards west since Arbroath's world record scoreline.*

Glebe Park

Brechin City

Brechin Harp and Brechin Hearts amalgamated in 1906 to form Brechin City FC, but the club didn't take up residence at Glebe Park until 1919.

In those days, the ground had just one stand, a portable affair previously used at Perth Agricultural Show. But, famously, Glebe Park did (and still does) have a hedge along one side of the ground instead of a wall.

It remains the only stadium boundary hedge in world football, but has been controversial in the past.

In 2009, UEFA decreed that every pitch in every league in the European football structure had to be a minimum of 70 yards wide. Glebe Park's playing surface is only 67 yards.

It couldn't be widened because Brechin didn't own the land beyond the hedge, and on the other side the stand is close to the touchline. It seemed an insoluble problem so the European governing body eventually decided to forget the notion – but not before the hedge had made headlines worldwide, representing a David-like character in a struggle against Goliath UEFA.

■ *The stand, left, and the famous hedge, right, in 1949 when it was little more than a shrub.*

■ *Glebe Park's record attendance is 8,123 for a cup tie with Aberdeen in 1973. It was the third-last ground in Scotland (in 1977) to get floodlights.*

PENSIONERS & JUVENILES 1/6

■ *Three youngsters about to pay their 1/6 (7½ p) to go through the turnstiles at Glebe Park in the 1960s. Entry for adults was 3/- (15p).*

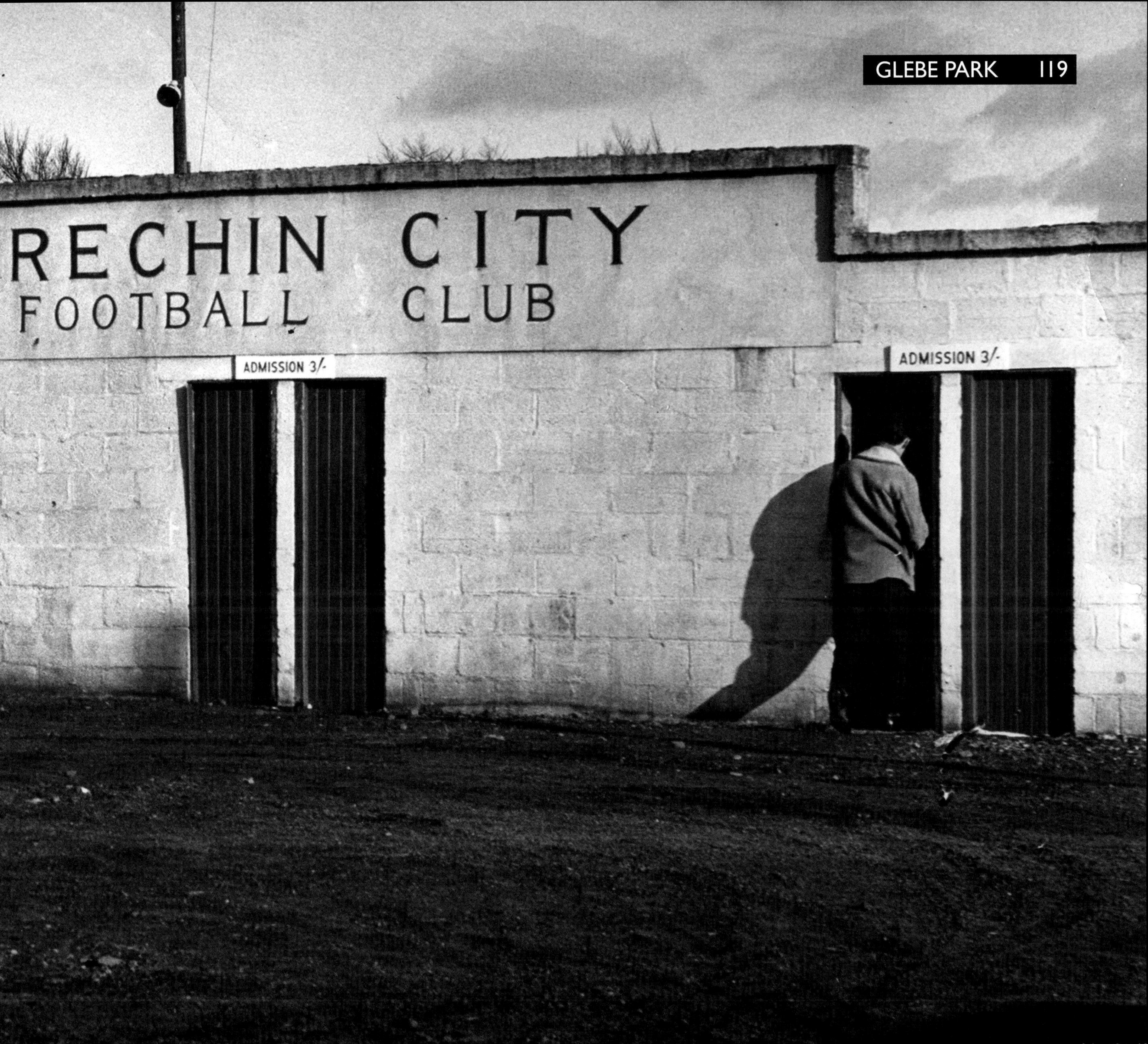
RECHIN CITY
FOOTBALL CLUB
ADMISSION 3/-
ADMISSION 3/-

Hampden

Queen's Park & Scotland

The Hampden Park of today, the stadium we've known since 1903, is the third Hampden.

Queen's Park FC were formed in 1867, before the concept of a club owning its own ground, or even playing regularly at any one ground, was thought of. QPFC played wherever they could find a green piece of land in Glasgow before settling at the first Hampden in 1873. It is now a lawn bowling club at the junction of Queen's Drive and Cathcart Road.

With that ground threatened by the construction of a railway line, they moved to the second Hampden in 1884. This would go on to become Cathkin Park, home of Third Lanark. But Queen's, the dominant force in Scottish football at the time, outgrew this too. When the land owners refused permission for further development the club again sought a new home.

In November 1899 a site at Somerville Drive, a few hundred yards south, was purchased and construction of a giant began. It took four years to build, to a design by the famous Archibald Leitch.

The first Ibrox disaster, in 1902, resulted in a change to the construction work. The problem at Ibrox had been a collapse of wooden terracing held up by scaffolding. To avoid a repetition, the terraces at Hampden were set in earthwork, with Leitch's invention of surge barriers installed to keep the sways of the crowd in check.

■ *Hampden in 1970, still the highest capacity in Europe.*

In 1903 the wonder of the age, the largest football stadium anywhere in the world, was unveiled. Hampden would retain that title until 1950.

Queen's Park, however, had steadfastly remained amateur, so the calibre of player they could attract was limited. The crowds watching the successful professional teams showed no sign of lessening.

Evening Telegraph, October 29, 1903

THE NEW QUEEN'S PARK ENCLOSURE

THE opening of Queen's Park's colossal ground this weekend marks a new era in Scottish football.

'How to build a football enclosure large enough to hold international crowds' is the question that has harassed Queen's Park, Celtic, and Rangers in turn; how to get crowd large enough to fill New Hampden will be the problem of the future.

There is nothing like the new ground in the Kingdom. Even when told that operations have been in progress for over two years, that £30,000 has been spent in housing 100,000 spectators, and that ever so many thousand feet of timber has been used building up the terraces and forming the barriers, one can have no conception of the new ground.

It must be seen to realised; a 30,000 crowd will appear a mere fringe, and an ordinary Hampden crowd will scarcely be discernible in that valley where but lately ran the Malls Mire, but now reduced to mere bricked-up sewer.

Ibrox and Parkhead have had their day; henceforth Hampden will be the Mecca of international pilgrims. The covered stand, the steepest of its kind on any football ground, will be ready for the opening match, and a temporary structure has been erected for the accommodation of Lord Provost Primrose and other invited guests.

■ *The double life of Hampden has always confused non-Scots. Why does an amateur club have a vast stadium that is all but deserted for their own games (left)? But full to the gunnels for other matches (right)? The answer can only be found if you study the history.*

■ *Rangers v. Dundee in the League Cup Final of 1951 at a packed Hampden.*

■ *Hampden in the 1920s.*

■ *Hampden in 1961.*

The enormous floodlight pylons at Hampden were first used in 1961. Rangers played Eintracht Frankfurt in a friendly that set one of Hampden's many records. The crowd for the game, on October 17, was 104,494 – the highest attendance for any friendly ever staged in Britain.

Hampden hosted a crowd of 136,505 for the Celtic v. Leeds United European Cup semi-final on April 15, 1970 – the biggest ever crowd for any European tie in any competition.

The greatest crowd to see a game between two clubs, at the time, was the Aberdeen v. Celtic Scottish Cup Final of 1937, attended by 144,303, or 147,365, depending on which source you believe. Either figure was easily a world record. There was also, according to reports, another 20,000 outside who couldn't get in.

Queen's Park made further improvements after the 1937 cup final which, they said, would allow crowds above 188,000, but the police refused to sanction such numbers.

The first turnstiles were used at Hampden, as were the first season tickets.

The reputation of the famous 'Hampden Roar' sprung to life in 1929 after a Home International against England. Scotland had been reduced to 10 men when Huddersfield Town winger Alex Jackson (formerly of Dumbarton and Aberdeen) was carried off injured.

The Scots equalised in the last minute when inside-forward Alex Cheyne curled a corner directly into the net. Jackson, by then in the A&E department at Glasgow Victoria Infirmary a full mile away, knew Scotland had scored from the noise. Newspapers reported him hearing 'the roar' and an enduring legend was born.

SECTION D WEST
SEATS 1-32

SECTION D EAST
SEATS 34-65
Entrance →

■ *The two towers of Hampden's grand main entrance in 1985. They were part of the 1937 redesign of the stadium.*

■ *The press box atop Hampden's main stand in 1966. It sloped at an alarming degree that always disconcerted first-timers.*

In her later years, the grand dame of world football stadiums began to look her age. Capacity was reduced to 135,000 in 1949 for safety reasons and a year later Hampden lost the title of 'world's biggest football stadium' when Rio de Janeiro unveiled the Estadio do Maracana for the World Cup of 1950.

A cover was put over the West Terrace, known as 'The Rangers End', in 1967 but the cost of building it put Queen's Park into debt and struggling to make any further improvements that might have prolonged the old stadium's life.

Various revamp schemes were proposed, including taking Hampden into public ownership – a notion which didn't please the QP board one bit.

In 1978 there was a glimmer of hope, with the SFA gaining the backing of Scotland's league clubs to rebuild with the help of the then Labour Government to meet the projected £11 million cost. But Margaret Thatcher's sweep to power a year later put a stop to that.

It took another 20 years, several false starts, trips up blind alleys and cost overruns, before the 'new' all-seater Hampden emerged just in time for the 1999 Scottish Cup Final.

■ *A rear view of the North Enclosure in 1981. By then it was little more than a crumbling, foreboding ruin.*

■ *The fateful moment. Santini's header crashes off the underside of Hampden's square crossbar and rebounds into play.*

For reasons no one left alive knows, square goalposts were normal in Scotland in the black & white era, although almost everyone else in world football used round or eliptical ones.

It was never a controversial matter.

Indeed, until 1978 there was no rule on what shape a goalpost should be. So for the 1976 European Cup Final, between French club St Etienne and Bayern Munich, the posts at Hampden stayed as they were. No one had any suspicion they were about to pass into European football lore.

St Etienne lost 1-0 to the German giants, who had the formidable Franz Beckenbauer, Gerd Muller and Sepp Maier in their line-up.

But French supporters are convinced that had the crossbar been round, then Jacques Santini's header and Dominique Bathenay's shot would have scraped into the net rather than both efforts rebounding from the sharp edges of the angular frame.

This festered with the French club and in 2013 when the Scottish Football Museum auctioned Hampden's old goalposts (which had been in place from 1903 until the rule change in 1978) St Etienne bought them for 20,000 euros. They stand in the club's museum at their ground, *the Stade Geoffroy Guichard* – blamed and cursed to this day for their part in denying *Les Verts* (The Greens) a European Cup win.

The phrase *les poteaux carres* (the square posts) is still used as an expression of bad luck in the French city.

Ibrox

Rangers

■ *The high-capacity bowl that Ibrox was in the early 1960s.*

Rangers were formed in 1872 by a group of rowing enthusiasts who were looking for another sporting pastime.

Legend has it that one of the founders, Moses McNeil, suggested the name after reading about a team called Swindon Rangers in a book on English rugby.

The fledgling club played their first games at Glasgow Green, north of the Clyde and, like most clubs, played at various venues in those early years. The first regular ground was at Burnbank in 1875. They then played at Clydesdale cricket ground in West Scotland Street from 1876 to 1887, but never actually owned the land.

In any case, more room for spectators was needed. The club was almost instantly successful.

The move to the first Ibrox Park took potential attendances up, but by 1899 a new ground with room for an even higher capacity was again urgently required. The second, and current, Ibrox slightly overlaps the footprint of the old ground, which bordered Copland Road.

The Ibrox of the 1920s was an oval shape with a pavilion housing the offices and changing rooms and a grandstand along one side. It held about 40,000 but in those days Ibrox, Celtic Park and Hampden competed to host international matches and cup finals, which could generate significant revenue. Ibrox added large terracing structures behind first the west, then the east ends of the ground, taking capacity up to 75,000.

These terraces, made of wooden planks bolted to ironwork scaffolds, weren't trusted after the Ibrox disaster of 1902 so were replaced by vast mounds of earth. By 1910 Ibrox could hold 63,000 spectators.

■ *A packed Ibrox in 1962, showing the magnificent main stand opened in 1929. It is generally regarded as the high point of famed football grounds architect Archibald Leitch's grandstand-designing career.*

By the early part of the 20th Century, Glasgow had the world's three biggest purpose-built football stadiums.

The Main Stand at Ibrox, with the famous red-brick façade, was built in 1928 and opened on January 1, 1929. It had 10,000 seats.

The height of the other three terraces kept being increased throughout the 1930s until, on January 2, 1939, Ibrox recorded Britain's highest ever crowd for a league game. The New Year Old Firm encounter drew 118,567 and saw the home side win 2-1.

■ *Left: Ibrox was the first stadium in Glasgow to install drenchlighting. The lights were inaugurated with a friendly against Arsenal on December 8, 1953. The first illuminated league game was on March 7, 1956, an 8-0 victory over Queen of the South.*

■ *Right: The main entrance at Ibrox pictured in 1962.*

The wrought iron gates of Ibrox, made to a design by Leitch, are one of the ground's most famous features. Few visitors from overseas leave without a photo of themselves with the gates in the background.

The gates are now at the corner of the Broomloan Road and Main Stands, but were originally erected at the Copland Road end.

Any book about old football stadiums must pay respects to supporters who lost their lives in those stadiums, and the families of those supporters.

The 1902, 1961 and 1971 Ibrox tragedies must never be forgotten. During a Scotland-England match in 1902, 25 supporters were killed when a section of terracing collapsed. In 1961, two people were killed in a crush on Stairway 13. In 1971, again on Stairway 13, 66 died after a Rangers-Celtic match.

This book is a celebration of the grounds of the past, but also offers sympathies for those who set off to attend an ordinary event, a football match, but never came home.

That shouldn't have happened.

There have been deaths at other grounds, too.

The victims of all three Ibrox accidents are listed on blue plaques beneath the statue of legendary club captain John Greig.

Ibrox has become one of Europe's great football stadiums.

The red-brick frontage on Edmiston Drive, again designed by Archibald Leitch, is a Category B listed building. This means it is a 'building of regional or more than local importance' and consent must be sought from the local authority before any alterations can be made.

Rangers put an upper deck on what was by then called the Bill Struth Main Stand in 2006, to mark the 50th anniversary of their celebrated manager's death.

■ *Right: The view from Edmiston Drive in 1962.*

READY

Ibrox today is unrecognisable from the old ground, having been almost completely remodelled from the late 1970s onward.

Willie Waddell, former player and team manager, who also served as general manager and vice-chairman is credited as the driving force behind the modern all-seater stadium. In the aftermath of the 1971 Ibrox Disaster he visited Borussia Dortmund's Westfalenstadion and took inspiration for the new Ibrox.

The curved ends were replaced by the near-identical Copland Road and Broomloan Road stands. The Centenary Stand was replaced by the Govan Stand (now the Sandy Jardine Stand).

Never again would crowd safety be compromised at Ibrox.

■ *Ibrox in the early 1960s.*

Links Park

Montrose

Montrose have played at Links Park since 1887, the club having been formed eight years earlier in 1879. They are the second oldest club in Angus, just a year younger than bitter rivals Arbroath.

Life was tough in the club's early years. To raise money they rented out their pitch to circuses, for grazing livestock and even for women's football. The club was so poor it had to borrow cash to afford goal nets when they became compulsory for the beginning of the 1891-92 season.

For more than 30 years, there was standing room-only at Links Park – there was no place to sit. But a solution was found in November 1921. The local paper reported 'an excellent temporary expedient for overcoming the difficulties created by the absence of a grandstand at Links Park and incidentally adding to their revenues a little, by securing the loan of the forms, etc, used as a grandstand at Montrose Highland Games.'

It was officially opened with a visit from Queen's Park Strollers for the first home game of 1922.

■ *Links Park's Wellington Street End (known as the Dynamo End to Gable Endies) was given a roof, and had its terraced banking built up, in 1963.*

Montrose's first ground was closer to the sea and known as 'the Metally', thanks to its proximity to the Metal Bridge.

Their next ground was close to Dorward House, before a move to the first Links Park, on the north side of what is now Dorward Road, in 1885.

The second, and current, Links Park saw its record crowd of 8,983 in 1973, for the visit of Dundee FC.

■ *Police keep an eye on the crowd at Links Park for Montrose's Scottish Cup quarter-final against Dundee in 1973. A degree of displeasure at the scoreline (Dundee won 4-1) had resulted in some unrest.*

Love Street

St Mirren

St Mirren were formed in 1877 and, like all
football clubs, played on various parks as they
established themselves.

In the early years of the game, teams didn't
run offices or have buildings at their 'home' pitch,
or – much of the time – even have the facility to
enclose the field in order to charge for admission.
Clubs slowly evolved to the point they could
justify a permanent base, and have a need for
raised areas which could fit more people in behind
those at pitch-side. Only then did grounds as we
understand them begin to emerge.

In Paisley, this happened fairly early.
St Mirren was already a gentlemen's sports
club, playing cricket and rugby, and they took
up association football too. The footballers were
founder members of the Scottish League system in
1890 and in 1895 took up residence at St Mirren
Park, a former brickworks. It was titled Fullerton
Park after the landowner, but became commonly
referred to as Love Street.

The club completed the purchase of the land
in 1920 and the main stand was finished in 1921,
having been under construction for almost 10
years. Like many football grounds, the terraces
were built up over the course of several years,
having railway sleepers (purchased at sixpence
each) laid on top of rubble dumped by the public.

■ *St Mirren Park, and surroundings, in 1951.*

There was a problem installing floodlights at Love Street in the 1950s as the ground was close to the flightpath of what was, at that time, Glasgow Airport at Abbotsinch.

The difficulty was overcome by putting in extremely low (compared to most other football grounds) pylons, which were unpopular with players and fans alike.

From the spartan origins, however, a ground emerged that the club's directors claimed had a capacity of 70,000 (although the highest attendance recorded is 47,438 in 1949).

St Mirren played at Love Street on the famously large pitch (it was 120 yards long at some points in its history – Hampden is only 115 yards) until 2009, when a deal struck with Tesco paid for a new stadium and cleared the club's debts.

The last game at the old Love Street was a 0-0 draw with Motherwell on January 3, 2009, in front of a sell-out crowd.

The club moved less than a mile to the new St Mirren Park at Greenhill Road.

■ *The old main stand at Love Street.*

Muirton

St Johnstone

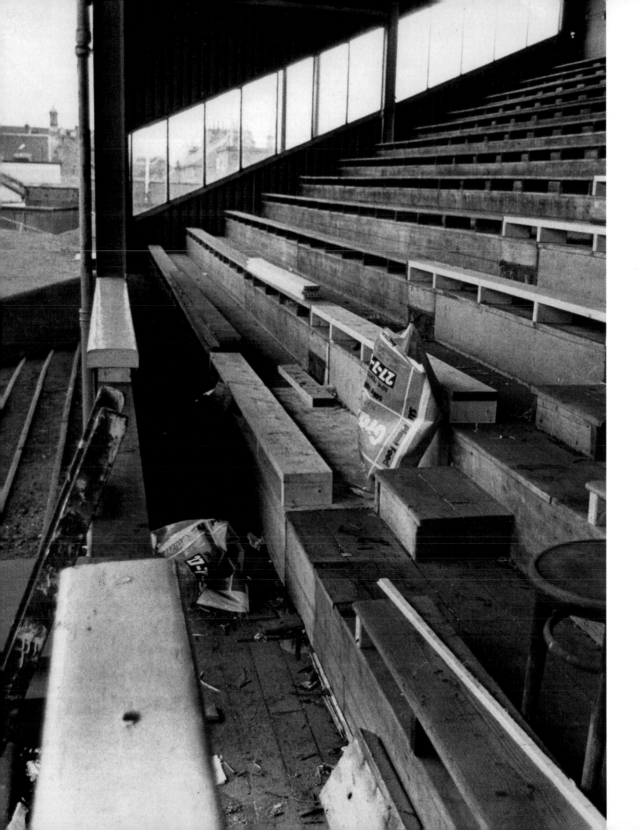

St Johnstone spent nearly 40 years, after their formation in 1885, playing at the Recreation Grounds opposite Perth Prison.

But success, and the securing of Scottish Football League status in 1911, made it apparent that a new stadium was required. The Saintees selected a piece of ground close to the Dunkeld Road (usefully on the tram routes) which had enough room to construct a playing surface of international standards and dimensions.

It was the accepted layout for the time, a wooden grandstand with three sides of banked terracing. A roof was added to the east terracing in the early 1950s and a record crowd of almost 30,000 attended a Scottish Cup tie with Dundee on February 10, 1951.

St Johnstone have won the Scottish second tier league (under its various names since the 1893-94 season) seven times – a record they share with Falkirk.

■ *Work being done on the stand in the early 1980s, towards the end of Muirton's service to the Saints.*

■ *The crowd in the main stand for a match with Aberdeen on January 2, 1969.*

By the 1980s Muirton was becoming a little frayed at the edges. Capacity went down to 11,500, with (for safety reasons) only 500 allowed into a stand that had 2,185 seats. Trouble loomed.

But three shining knights came along. The first was shrewd local businessman Geoff Brown, who provided nous and capital, the second was farmer Bruce McDiarmid, who provided 16 acres of land. The third was supermarket chain Asda, who also liked the look of the Dunkeld Road position the ground enjoyed – even if the trams no longer ran.

They put up a supermarket, St Johnstone put up the first purpose-built all-seater football stadium in the UK.

The club moved out of Muirton and into McDiarmid Park in 1989.

■ *Perth enjoys one of the milder climates in Scotland... but not all the time. This pitch-sanding photo is from 1968.*

■ *Right: Muirton got floodlights in 1964.*

New Kilbowie

Clydebank

Clydebank Juniors played at the original Kilbowie, closer to the river than 'New Kilbowie' which was bought in 1937. It holds the distinction of being the first ground in Scotland to have round, instead of the traditional square, goalposts.

The town's former league club (also called Clydebank, but no relation) participated in the Scottish League system from 1914 to 1931 but then folded. The junior club had ambitions to better themselves, so, keen to have a football club, the town council helped with the cost of setting up New Kilbowie, which opened in 1939.

However, Clydebank was terribly damaged by bombing raids in 1941. The ground escaped relatively unscathed, but the surroundings were devastated.

Once league status was achieved, the ground went from strength to strength. There were various upgrades and in 1977 the Bankies won promotion to the Premier Division. However, all Scottish top flight grounds had to comply with the Safety of Sports Grounds Act if they held more than 10,000 spectators. The changes required would have been expensive, so to keep capacity below 10k, 9,950 seats (mostly benches) were installed, making New Kilbowie the first all-seated football ground in Britain.

Clydebank went into decline and in 1996 sold New Kilbowie. The promised replacement stadium was never built, forcing ground-shares with Dumbarton, then Morton. The club went into administration and was wound up in 2002.

■ *New Kilbowie Park in 1964.*

In an unusual and ambitious move, Clydebank attempted to inject a cafe culture aspect in September 1967.

Patrons of the social club (which claimed a membership of 1,000 with twice as many on the waiting list) could be served drinks during games.

The list of Parisian-style street table ventures in the history of Scottish football is short and, in truth, this example didn't last long either.

But it was an interesting time to live in Clydebank. With worldwide attention and great local celebration the QE2 was about to be launched from the John Brown & Co. shipyard. The town had a buzz about it.

The Steedman brothers, Jack and Charlie, had merged their club East Stirlingshire with Clydebank in 1965 and made Kilbowie the home pitch.

That arrangement lasted only a year before a legal challenge separated the clubs again. But the Steedmans stayed at Clydebank, who gained league status in their own right in 1966, and injected energy and ideas in a determined effort to make a success of the club.

Ochilview

Stenhousemuir

The Warriors were formed in 1894 in a breakaway from another team, Heather Rangers. They have played at Ochilview, named for its view of the Ochil Hills, since 1890.

The Doll's House stand was built in 1928 to replace Stenhousemuir's previous stand which had been badly damaged by a fire earlier the same year. The name reflected the compact nature of the construction.

It had to have two external staircases, added later – when it was realised that the original design hadn't included any way for spectators to get to their seats.

It was demolished in 1999, when it was finally refused a safety certificate.

■ *Left – The Doll's House stand from behind and, right, the rest of the ground in 1971.*

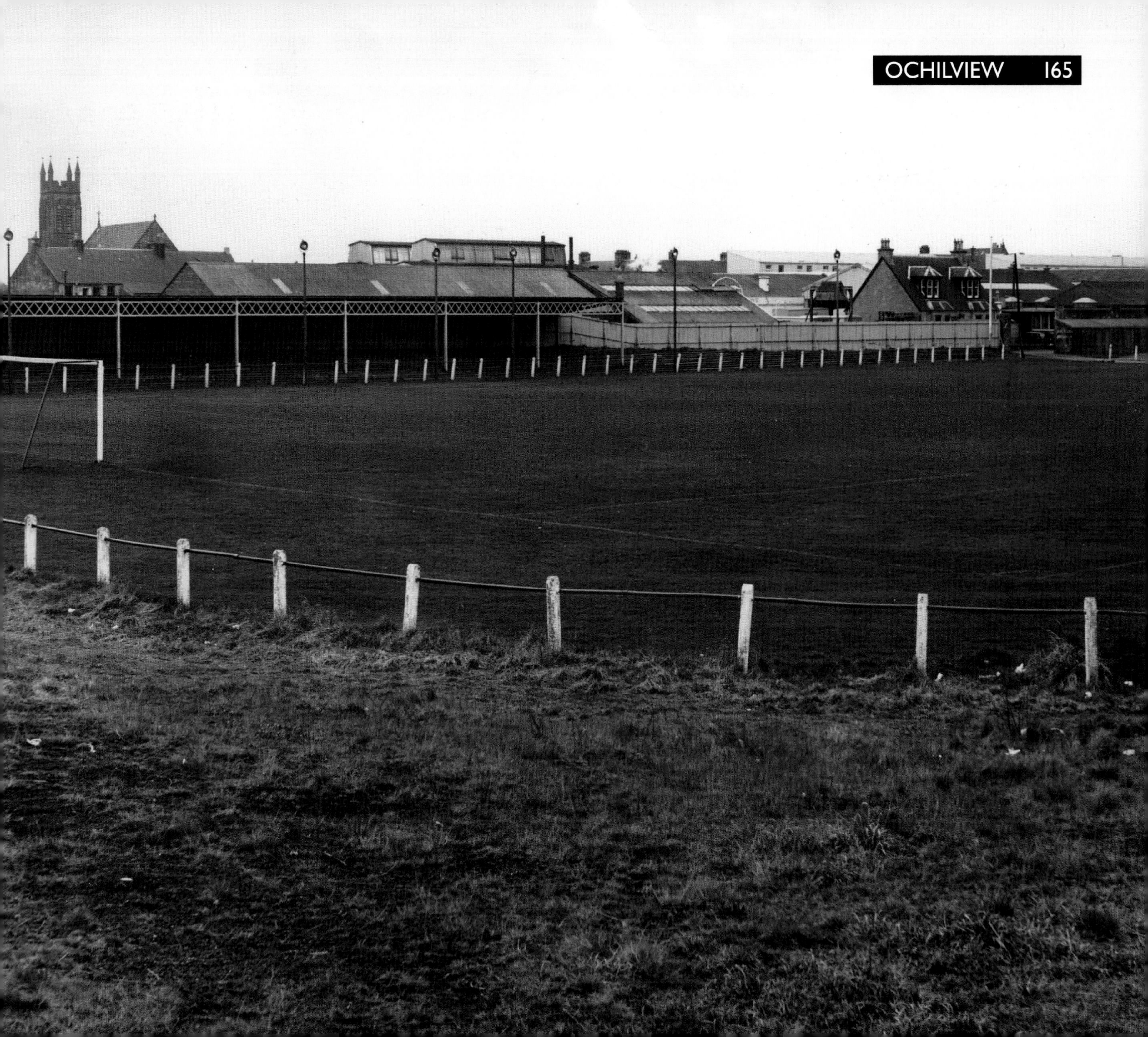

The light of achievement shines on Ochilview because of a remarkable and ground-breaking move for Scottish football.

It was the venue for the very first floodlit match in the country, a friendly with Hibs on November 7, 1951. And the shining light of a new era caused a stir throughout the land.

Dundee Courier, November 7, 1951

SPOTLIGHT ON FLOODLIGHT

The football spotlight is on floodlight tonight. There will be two games under the arcs, one in Paris between Arsenal and Racing Club, and in Scotland the experiment is being tried out at Ochilview Park by Stenhousemuir and Hibs.

All leading Scottish club officials' have been invited to Stenhousemuir so that they can see for themselves the possibilities of this venture.

They will report back to their clubs. We may then see a feverish installing of lights at many grounds or we may get a verdict that such a development is unsuitable for our Scottish climate.

Seven thousand five hundred tickets have been sold for this game. There'll be turnstiles for cash customers up to another 3500. An aggregate crowd of 11,000 is being arranged for. Holding capacity of this ground is 15,000.

As all branches of the Hibs Supporters Club received a ticket allocation, the Easter Road side will not lack support.

It was officially stated last night that the heavy rain would not affect the ground, said to be one of the best drained pitches in Scotland.

Kick-off is at 7 p.m.

Crowd Scenes

In the early years of Scottish football, the 1910s and 1920s when football stadiums as we recognise them were emerging, the emphasis was on capacity. Clubs tried to make them as big as possible to cater for the incredible numbers who wanted to attend matches.

Hampden, Ibrox, Celtic Park, Tynecastle, Firhill, Douglas Park and Cappielow all had their biggest ever crowds in the 1930s. There was another boom after the Second World War. Easter Road, Dens, Pittodrie, Fir Park, Brockville, Stark's Park and many more saw their largest attendances in the 1950s.

Hibs had ambitions to take Easter Road's capacity above 100,000, East Fife had plans for a stadium in Methil that would hold 35,000.

It could be argued that there wasn't much in the way of alternative entertainment, or that admission prices in those days were more affordable. But no matter how you look at it, football was phenomenally popular. No other sport comes close.

If those were the halcyon days of crowds, then they must also be regarded as the halcyon days of football stadiums.

Will we ever see images like these again?

■ *Dundee's Dens Park surrounded by supporters trying to get in before kick-off for a game against Rangers in 1947.*

Any perch to get a view...even on the billboards at Dens Park.

■ *The Scottish Cup being paraded, on a modified tea trolley, round Brockville in 1957. As was customary in any big crowd in the 1950s, children were sent to the front and would watch the match, or cup parade, from the cinder track. Falkirk took armies of supporters to Hampden for the cup final and replay. The Saturday 1-1 draw was watched by 81,375, while the replay the following Wednesday, April 24, was attended by a quite incredible 79,960.*

Any account of attendances in Scotland must acknowledge the extraordinary pulling power of The Old Firm. Most other Scottish clubs' attendance records are in matches against one or other of the Glasgow giants, thanks to their huge travelling supports.

The 95,722 who saw Queen's Park entertain Rangers in 1930 is still the world record for a game involving an amateur team. The 147,365 at the Celtic v. Aberdeen Scottish Cup Final of 1937 is a European record for a domestic match.

The Old Firm's attendance records are, of course, against each other. A crowd of 118,567 (a British record for a league game) were at Ibrox for the 1939 New Year encounter, while 92,975 were at Celtic Park for Rangers' visit in January 1938.

The largest Old Firm attendance was 132,870 at Hampden for the 1969 Scottish Cup Final.

The highest European Cup Final attendance was 127,621 for the Real Madrid rout of Eintracht Frankfurt in 1960.

Scotland is the world's 119th most populous nation. But when it comes to football crowds, we are ranked No. 1.

■ *Left: The Celtic-Rangers record crowd at Hampden in 1969.*

The record attendance at Dunfermline's East End Park was recorded on April 30, 1968, the last day of the 1967-68 league season.

The Pars had won the Scottish Cup three days previously and a crowd of 27,816 squeezed in for the visit of Celtic.

The Glasgow club needed a win or a draw to be mathematically assured of the league title, although it would have taken an unlikely score in Dunfermline's favour to rob them of it as an Aberdeen win over Rangers, on the same day Pars won the cup, had all but ended the Ibrox challenge

It was a chaotic day. The fans were so tightly packed that crush barriers were buckled out of shape. Anyone who ever saw a crush barrier will appreciate they took quite an amount of force to bend.

■ *Left: The game got under way with spectators seeking any vantage point they could cling to.*

■ *Right: Some of the bent and buckled barriers and perimeter fencing after the game.*

Kick-off was delayed and spectators spilled on to the pitch, climbed floodlight pylons and on to the terracing roof to see the action.

One man, named at the time as William Brown, of Whiteinch, Glasgow, died of head injuries after reportedly falling from the terracing roof.

Another 49 people were injured, 16 seriously enough to require hospital treatment.

The game, which took place on a Wednesday night, was stopped after 20 minutes of play, with the players taken off the pitch. It was resumed nine minutes later.

■ *Left: With a backdrop of fans lining the terrace roof, match referee Tiny Wharton consults with police and officials over whether to remove the players from the pitch.*

■ *Right: Spectators ripped up anything they could find in an attempt to create makeshift extra steps of terracing.*

Palmerston

Queen of the South

Queen of the South have played at the same ground in Dumfries, not far from the river Nith, since they came into existence in 1919. The ground is situated on land that used to form part of a farm known as Palmers Toun.

The club was the amalgamation of three teams: Dumfries FC, The 5th King's Own Scottish Borderers football team and the Arrol-Johnston Car Company's team.

The town of Dumfries had been called 'the queen of the south' by David Dunbar, a poet and prospective parliamentary candidate, in a speech in 1857. The nickname stuck and the newly-formed club took it as their title. They should not, however, be confused with Queen of the South Wanderers FC who existed from 1873 to 1894.

Palmerston was the first choice but Queens were unable to just walk in and take over. It belonged to the 5th KOSB and, although they used it for football, it was also their parade ground. There was a back-up plan – Nunholm Park, over the Nith and further out of town – and for a while it looked like Plan B might have to be put into use as it was taking time to receive a response from Major Frazer, commanding officer of the 5th KOSB.

However, Major Frazer eventually decided the club could become tenants of Palmerston from May 1, 1919, at £10 per year – but only on condition the regiment would have the privilege of the field if there was a military emergency. Luckily, no military emergencies have arisen in Dumfries – so far – that have been serious enough to interfere with the football.

■ *Palmerston in 1933, with a stand that was 'too far away from the pitch'.*

■ *In 1927 a major operation got under way to level the Palmerston pitch. The Terregles Street end was smoothed out with soil from the other end of the stadium. Picture © Ian McCartney.*

In 1921 QoS sold Jimmy McKinnell, Tom Wylie and Willie McCall to Blackburn Rovers, and Ian Dickson to Aston Villa. This raised enough money to fund the £1,500 purchase of Palmerston from the Army, who had to make other arrangements for their response to any invasion of Dumfries.

With ownership confirmed, a new grandstand was built at a cost of £820 in time for the 1921-22 season. The stand was 120 feet long, with seven rows and sat 600 to 650 spectators – though it attracted complaints that it was too high at the front and too far from pitch-side.

That original stand burned down in 1965 but was swiftly replaced by the larger construction that remains in place today.

Palmerston is, technically, in Maxwelltown, although Maxwelltown became part of Dumfries in 1929.

Palmerston's floodlight pylons, erected in 1958, are the tallest free-standing floodlights left in Scottish football at 85 feet. They were among the first Scottish clubs to erect pylons, it being more usual to attach lights to the roofs of grandstands.

Pittodrie

Aberdeen

The current Aberdeen Football Club is the result of a 1903 three-way amalgamation of the original Aberdeen FC and clubs called Victoria United and Orion. Pittodrie had been home to the old Aberdeen FC. They were founded in 1881 and had played at various venues around the city until 1899, when Pittodrie became their permanent home.

The land had been an army shooting range and, legend has it, a dung hill for the horses of Aberdeen's police force, but was cleared and a pitch laid.

The area was also, reputedly, once named Gallows Marsh and had been the city's venue for public executions.

However, one of the great stadiums of Scottish football grew on the shores of the North Sea.

In 1908 it was the last senior ground in Britain to cease giving free admission to women.

The main stand was built in 1925, along with the impressive granite gates at the Merkland Road End.

By 1978 all three terraces were roofed and Pittodrie became the UK's first all-seater stadium.

But while it holds fantastic memories for the Red Army of Dons supporters, time marches on and requirements change. It may soon be consigned to history as the club are close to a move to a new stadium.

■ *Pittodrie in the 1950s.*

■ *Donald Colman in his days as a Dons player.*

Pittodrie holds a unique place in the history of football grounds. It was the first in the world to have dugouts.

They were the invention of original-thinker Donald Colman, Aberdeen FC captain and later coach. Colman was a genius. He was interested in dancing and applied his knowledge of the way the human body moves to football. He paid great attention to the use of space and the footwork of his players to get into and create room for themselves.

To better observe what was happening on the pitch, Colman required to be close to it. In the days before substitutes, fourth officials and pitchside TV reporters, most managers and coaches sat in the grandstands and observed their teams from there. Requiring a place out of the rain to take his meticulous notes, Colman had dugouts created in the early 1930s. Everton visited for a friendly, liked the idea, copied it – and soon every club had dugouts.

Aberdeen Evening Express, May 30, 1959

ABERDEEN soccer enthusiasts will see the Dons in action under floodlights at Pittodrie Park during the coming season.

It was announced yesterday that the Aberdeen club had decided to fall into line with the majority of Scottish First Division clubs and install a lighting system.

The project will be started in the immediate future and is expected to be ready for the early starts in October. The work will be carried out by an Aberdeen firm and the pylon system of lighting the ground will be adopted.

It is estimated that the installation will cost in the region of £12,000 or £15,000. With Aberdeen joining Celtic and Dunfermline in deciding to turn on the lights next season, only half-a-dozen Scottish First Division clubs will be without an artificial lighting system.

The following official statement was issued by Mr C. B. Forbes, Aberdeen F.C. vice-chairman.

"The directors have decided to give the go-ahead for floodlighting at Pittodrie Park. Their planning has been on the principle that covered accommodation should have priority and now this had been accomplished on a scale far greater than by any other provincial club they are to concentrate on an efficient system for lighting Pittodrie.

The matter has been given careful consideration for some time and various forms of illumination have been examined.

The directors are pleased to announce that the order for floodlighting the ground will be placed with Aberdeen firm of Claud Hamilton (Aberdeen) Ltd.

"They would be responsible for the whole of the work, and with co-operation from the North of Scotland Hydro Board and the local authority, the system should be ready by the time lights are required this year.

"The firm had made an extensive study of the problem, which differs for every ground, and had recommended the pylon type of lighting, with four towers. Two of the towers would be at each end of the main stand, and would be 120 feet high, and the two corresponding towers on top of the main

terracing would be approximately the same height from ground level.

"First the installation of floodlighting would ensure a 3 p.m. kick-off for all afternoon games, and postponed matches re-arranged for midweek could be played at night. Arrangements could also be made for a limited number of show games. Pittodrie Park would also come into the reckoning for representative matches, such as the under-23 internationals, and the ground would be available for practice games by the Aberdeen players."

There was a drop in attendances at Pittodrie last season, and while this could be traced, in part, to the Dons' poor showing in the league, the early start of games during October, November, December and January also had an adverse effect on the turn-out.

The majority of clubs with lighting adopted a 3 p.m. start during the winter months and played the second half under the arc lamps.

They were rewarded by increased attendances. There was a period when the Pittodrie officials were opposed to permitting the Dons to play under floodlights, but last term they relaxed their attitude and agreed to a second half light-up in several of their league fixtures away from home.

A crowd officially given as 40,00 squeezed in to Pittodrie for the first game, v. Hibs, of the new season after The Dons' glorious Scottish Cup win the previous April.

The cup had been won, coincidentally, also against Hibs 2-1, a Dons fightback after going behind in the first minute. This game, however, was a 2-0 win for Hibs.

Interestingly, it wasn't Aberdeen's first home game since winning the cup. The Scottish Cup Final hadn't been the climax of the season.

Aberdeen won at Hampden on April 19, 1947, but played a further six league games after that, including three at Pittodrie.

This was in large part due to the incredibly cold weather in the early months of 1947. It was so severe that Aberdeen played just one home league game (a 2-1 win over Clyde) between January 1 and May 3.

■ *Any viewpoint will do at the packed Aberdeen v. Hibs meeting to start the 1947-48 season.*

Recreation Park

Alloa Athletic

Alloa Athletic had quite a tour before settling at Recreation Park. They were at West End from their birth in 1878 until 1883. Then Gaberston Park for seven years, then Bellevue from 1890 before arriving at The Recs in 1895. And there they have stayed.

They also had a few different names. They were Clackmannan County for their first year, then Alloa Association Football Club for four years, before replacing Association with Athletic in 1883.

■ *Alloa v. Morton during The Wasps' promotion push in 1962.*

The Recs (as locals call it) is now the Indodrill Stadium. It had a charming wooden main stand, built in the 1920s, which was replaced in 1991 with a concrete construction. But in truth, apart from the roof supports, the new one looks a lot like the original.

Alloa were also fairly late putting in floodlights, not until 1979, making them the second last (only Stranraer held out longer) to let there be light.

The corrugated iron fence (once a common sight at grounds around Scotland) stayed for a long time too, not being replaced by a wall on the Clackmannan Road end until the 2007-08 season.

■ *Action from Alloa v. Stirling Albion in 1962, with a line of double-decker buses – the way all football supporters used to travel – in the car park. The clumps of long grass around the foot of the goalposts would be frowned upon in the modern game.*

Rugby Park

Kilmarnock

Kilmarnock are Scotland's oldest football club. They are so old, they almost pre-date football.

Killie were formed by members of a cricket team who wanted a sporting pastime to occupy them outwith their own season.

A meeting took place on January 5, 1869, and history was made – Scotland had a football team. Except they played rugby.

Until the Football Association started up in London in 1863, football didn't have agreed rules, every area had their own version that allowed various degrees of kicking, carrying the ball and what can only be described as 'vigorous' tackles.

The version the Killie cricketers played, was more like rugby. They adopted association football rules in 1873.

But the ground is still called Rugby Park – although it is their fifth ground.

The club played at The Grange, Holm Quarry and Ward's Park before moving to Rugby Park in 1877 – which wasn't the Rugby Park we know today. The original was close by on South Hamilton Street.

The final move, to the new and current Rugby Park, came in 1899.

© Kilmarnock FC

Like many early Scottish football grounds, Rugby Park had a pavilion where players and referee changed and the directors, the great and the good, sat. This was separate from Killie's long stand down one side, and the other three sides which were terraced.

The South Terrace got half of a roof in 1935 and, because of its large roof advert, became known as 'the Johnnie Walker'.

With football suspended, Rugby Park did its bit for the war effort in 1939 by becoming an army storage depot. Huge oil tanks on concrete foundations occupied the pitch. The playing surface had to be reinstated afterwards (although some of the concrete blocks only made it as far as the car park, where they stayed for several more years) and Italian prisoners of war were put to work to help build up the terracing banks again.

A new main stand was constructed over and around the old one in 1961. The stadium, with the driving forces of Bob Fleeting and Jim Moffat in the boardroom, was extensively reconstructed in 1994.

But there are no sheep any more.

For years, Rugby Park had a resident sheep as a mascot, but also with grass and weed-nibbling duties. There were three over the years, Angus, Ruby and Wilma.

■ *Killie players, including Frank Beattie, Andy Kerr and Jackie McInally, doing sprint training in front of the old west stand at Rugby Park in 1960. Tucked in the corner of the service tunnel wall, Angus the sheep runs his eye over their progress.*

Shawfield

Clyde

Clyde Football Club was founded in 1877 as a private members club and initially played at Barrowfield. They seem to have been an eclectic group of sportsmen who rowed, cycled and played tennis as well as kicked a ball.

The football side of the club, however, thrived. There was a huge appetite for the game in Glasgow towards the end of the 19th Century and Clyde became a victim of their own success. So much so that they outgrew the ground at Barrowfield, on the edge of Bridgeton. Many people were getting in to the ground without paying and the league had complaints from visiting teams about the poor facilities.

The club secured a former trotting track on land across the river at Shawfield and faced a huge task to transform it into a stadium in time for the 1898-99 football season. To raise money the club incorporated to become the Clyde Football Club Limited. A grandstand seating 1,500 was thrown up and embankments created around the pitch. The enthusiastic directors of the time estimated a final capacity of 100,000.

The period before World War 1 was a golden era for Clyde, with regular challenges for the league title and Scottish Cup Final appearances in 1910 and 1912.

■ *Left and right – Shawfield, complete with dog track, in 1950.*

A fire destroyed Shawfield's stand in 1914. Most of Clyde's early records were lost and there are no known surviving photos of the early years at Barrowfield.

The inter-war years saw success on the pitch, but struggles off it. To make ends meet, the club sold the ground to The Shawfield Greyhound Racing Company Ltd in 1935. The move solved short-term cash worries but created problems that lasted more than half a century. The football club would never again own Shawfield.

Following Clyde was rarely dull. There were relegations, promotions and cup wins in 1939, 1955 and 1958. But the slum clearances of Bridgeton, Gorbals and Oatlands decanted their local support to other parts of Glasgow, or the suburbs. They never really returned.

By the late 1970s Shawfield was owned by the Greyhound Racing Association and had fallen into sad disrepair. It was put up for sale in 1983 and Clyde were served notice to quit. The last Clyde game at Shawfield was April 28, 1986.

The unhappy years as a homeless entity, being tenants of Partick Thistle and sharing with Hamilton Accies, ended in 1994 when the club moved 15 miles to Cumbernauld and a new home at Broadwood.

■ *There are no balls in this picture. That's because it is pre-season training at Shawfield in 1938, when the emphasis was on fitness rather than skills.*

■ *In Shawfield's early years, plans had been put forward to build up the terraces until crowds of 100,000-plus could be accommodated. But with the development of Hampden, Celtic Park and Ibrox it was felt that Glasgow wouldn't require a fourth megastadium.*

Shielfield

Berwick Rangers

Berwick Rangers have been in existence since 1884, but lived a nomadic existence around the town – and played in several Scottish Borders and Northumberland league combinations – until settling at Shielfield Park. The only English club playing in Scotland joined the old Division B in 1955 (it was renamed Division Two a year later) and have been honorary Scotsmen ever since.

Despite not being the biggest club in the Scottish league system, The Wee Rangers reside in a wide open area on the Tweedmouth side of the river, on land formerly owned by local butcher William Shiel Dods, who gave his name to the ground.

The club's former pitch was immediately behind the current stadium on 'The Ducket' (Dovecote) enclosure side, opposite the main stand. It is still there and is used for training.

The Ducket is named for the many dovecotes behind the ground.

■ *Watching the Wee Rangers from The Ducket on a cold day in 1989, with police in English 'custodian helmets', rather than the caps a Scottish Bobby would wear. The custodian helmet doesn't seem to do much to keep policemen warm....*

In 1951, Berwick Rangers pulled off one of the more remarkable transfer deals in British football history. Due to the shortage of steel after the war, the club was finding it difficult to get their hands on any to build a stand with.

So they paid Bradford City, then in the English Division Three (North) £400 to buy the framework of Valley Parade's grandstand.

The Midland Road stand had been condemned by Bradford Corporation because the foundations were unsafe, but there was nothing wrong with the steelwork. It was dismantled and loaded on to a train for the 170-mile journey north.

British Railways shunted a train of specially converted wagons up the Kelso branch line next to Shielfield, where the dismantled sections were craned into place.

The pitch was completed with turf taken from land at the village of Beal a few miles south of Berwick at the closest mainland point to the Holy Island of Lindisfarne, possibly in an attempt to secure divine intervention for shots on goal.

■ *The imported-from-Bradford steel framework is put together at a bleak-looking Shielfield Park in 1951.*

© *Dennis McLeary*

Somerset Park

Ayr United

Ayr United is the only club in Scottish football history to be formed by the merger of two existing league clubs, Ayr FC and Ayr Parkhouse in 1910. Somerset Park had been home to Ayr FC since 1888.

Ayr FC previously played at Beresford Park, in the centre of town, and accepted an invitation to host a friendly against FA Cup holders Aston Villa. But Beresford Park was being used for Ayr Cattle Show, so the clubhouse and grandstand were hastily dismantled and re-erected across the river. And there they stayed.

Ayr formally purchased Somerset Park in 1920 and realigned the direction of the pitch when a new main stand was built. The structure still stands, one of the last Archie Leitch grandstands.

Somerset Park is, these days, hailed (and also complained about) as one of the last 'traditional' Scottish football grounds with its stand and three terraces.

■ *Somerset Park in 1977.*

AYR UNITED FC

ADMISSION   ADMISSION

The railway end terrace had a roof built over it in 1933 – and there is an enduring myth that it was split into male and female sections.

Sadly, it isn't true. In the 1930s Ayr United had a supporters' club for men and a separate supporters' club for women. In 1933, architect Charles Nair drew up a blueprint for an enclosure at the hitherto uncovered railway end and kindly donated the plans at no cost.

The bill for construction was an altogether different matter. A cheque for £130 was donated by the Ladies' Supporters Club and £230 by the (male) Supporters' Club. The enclosure (which still stands) was opened before a league fixture against Kilmarnock (a 1-1 draw) on September 30, 1933.

In his speech on the day, club director Alex Moffat jokingly said he hoped the respective supporters' clubs would continue to compete with each other in the matter of future donations.

This was the kernel from which the female/male areas story grew, but there was never more to it than that.

■ *Left, Somerset Park in 1952.*

■ *Right: Ayr v Motherwell in the Scottish Cup quarter-final of March 10, 1951, when 22,152 shoehorned themselves into Somerset Park.*

© *Duncan Carmichael*

Stair Park

Stranraer

The club was formed in 1870, making it the third oldest in Scottish football and putting it among the top 20 oldest clubs in the world.

In the early days they played at other venues in the town. Travel was difficult and there weren't many other teams in the area so there tended to be gaps between games until membership of various southern leagues brought more regular football.

Stranraer won a place in the Scottish C Division in 1949. Full league status of the B Division (soon to be the Scottish Second Division) followed in 1955.

Moving in to Stair Park wasn't straightforward. It is within a large park, which also has netball courts, a skatepark and large grassed areas, and was bequeathed to the town by the Earl of Stair in 1905. The club first played there in 1907 but the town council were initially opposed to the idea of enclosing an area and charging an entry fee to land that was technically owned by the townspeople.

The club put up a pavilion in 1909, as this was required to become an SFA member, but the right to fence off the ground wasn't sorted out until 1910.

The first real stand was put up in 1932 and stood until replaced with a cantilevered version in the 1990s. The Coo Shed, on the other side of the pitch, went up in the 1950s.

■ *The old wooden stand at Stair Park.*

© John Blair

Stark's Park

Raith Rovers

Raith Rovers were founded in 1883 and moved to Stark's Park (named after Councillor Robert Stark, owner of the land) in 1891. They transported the pavilion from their previous ground at Robbie's Park, a process that went well until an unfortunate height miscalculation at the railway bridge knocked several bits off it.

But room has always been an issue at Stark's Park. The Edinburgh-Aberdeen rail came through Kirkcaldy in 1847, while Pratt Street meanders up the hill narrowing the distance between road and rail line as it goes. Neither could be moved for the sake of association football.

The north end of Stark's Park fills every inch of the available space. There isn't even a pavement between the ground and the public highway. The tight site led to innovative measures. The main stand, built in 1925, stretched only to the halfway line – that's all there was room for. The Coo Shed on the opposite side was tucked in almost underneath the railway embankment, which gave the odd sensation of watching football while trains passed overhead.

But Rovers prospered. They were the first Fife club to enter the Scottish leagues, gaining membership in 1902. And, cramped or otherwise, a crowd of 31,036 managed to get inside Stark's Park for a cup-tie against Hearts in 1953.

■ *Stark's Park, squeezed by road and railway.*

■ *A roof being put over the Links Street end in August 1954. This is a good example of the ash-and-wood-slats terraces that were once common in football grounds.*

■ *March 4, 1956: Fans queue down Pratt Street, outside Stark's Park, for tickets to the Scottish Cup semi-final between Hearts and Rovers. The first game, at Easter Road, before a crowd of 58,448, was a 0-0 draw. Hearts won the replay the following Wednesday 3-0, again at Easter Road and this time before a crowd of 54,233, on their way to beating Celtic in the final that year. However, the semi-final was to prove uncomfortable, if not dangerous, for some supporters.*

The Sunday Post, March 25, 1956

CRUSHING WAS TERRIBLE, SAY FANS

THERE were angry demonstrations outside the main entrance of Easter Road football ground, Edinburgh, yesterday afternoon. Men, who were in the ground watching the Hearts v. Raith Rovers Scottish Cup semi-final, had to leave because of the crushing.

In all, several hundreds of spectators left the ground. Most of them went home.

Several dozen stayed on, however, and tried to make a protest to the management.

Just before half-time, police formed them into a queue and they were admitted to another part of the ground.

"It was terrible," said James Duncan, 65 Montrose Cottages, Lochore, Fife. "I felt my ribs were going to be broken any minute. It was impossible even to get my feet on the ground."

"I've never been in a crush like it. It was impossible to see the ball," said David McLean, 56 Windsor Park, Musselburgh.

Station Park
Forfar Athletic

■ *A full house for the Forfar v. Rangers Scottish Cup-tie of February 1958. A lone cameraman captures the action from the far side, while the buses that brought the huge Rangers travelling support are lined up in the background.*

Forfar Athletic were founded in 1885 when the second XI of Angus FC, also based in Forfar, broke away to form their own club. Station Park opened in 1888 and the club played in the various Angus and East of Scotland leagues of the early 20th Century before being admitted to the Scottish Football League system in 1921.

The ground once was, as the name suggests, close to the town's railway station but Dr Beeching's savage cuts of the 1960s left only the name intact.

Forfar had the rare distinction of The Duke of York (the future King George VI) and his wife (the future Queen Mother) attending one of their matches. The royal couple took in the Forfar v. Albion Rovers match on September 15, 1923.

The Duke had been given the freedom of the town of Forfar at a ceremony earlier in the day and, in truth, didn't make it to Station Park until after the second half had started.

He would no doubt have been cheered by The Loons' 3-1 victory, although failed to pay the admission fee – a debt that is still outstanding if his queenly daughter is reading this.

■ *The almost-complete, and built-in-a-hurry, new stand at Station Park on January 27, 1959.* Why was there such a rush? See page 58.

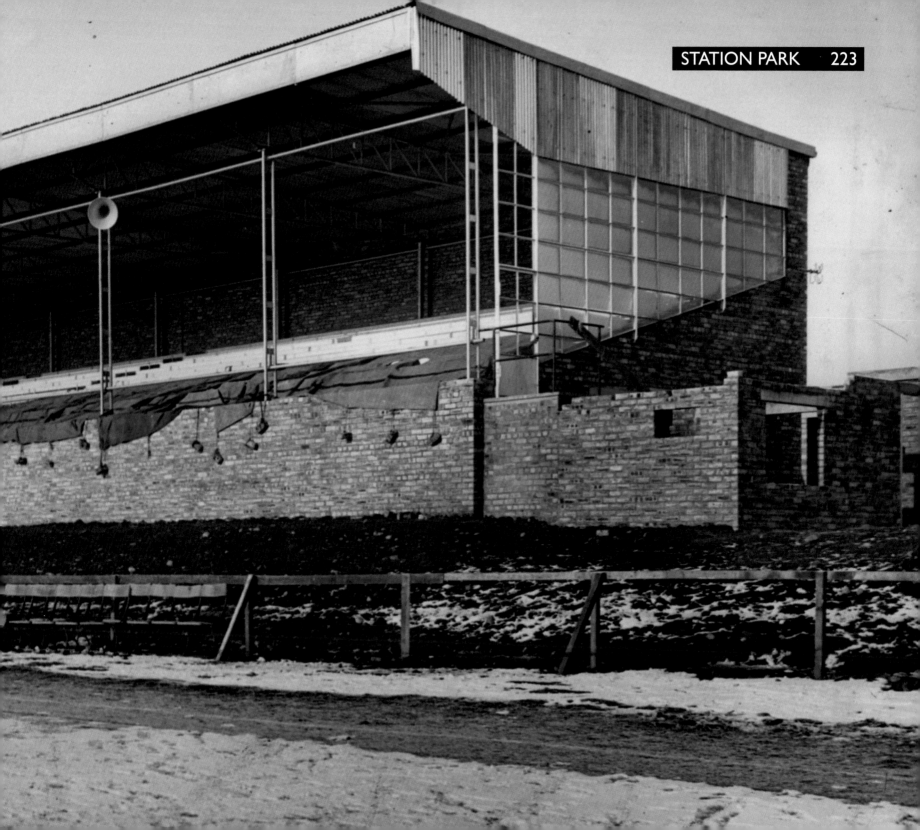

Tannadice

Dundee United

Dundee United were formed in 1909 by the amalgamation of several well-established football clubs in the town.

The new club represented the city's large Irish community, attracted to Dundee by the promise of employment in the jute mills, although the club never operated a sectarian signing policy. It was a surprise to many, however, that they didn't make their home in Dundee's western suburb of Lochee, where much of their support lived.

Clepington Park had been the home of Dundee Wanderers. When the Wanderers were told they were to be evicted they dismantled their grandstand and took away their goalposts. The new tenants were presented with an entirely vacant field without even proper fencing but they rebuilt and re-named it.

Tannadice Park grew from there.

■ *Left: The main stand and now-removed stand enclosure that made way for executive boxes and a widened pitch.*

■ *Tannadice has the unusual feature of a stand wider than its footprint. The back hangs over Tannadice Street.*

The old stand at Tannadice was a small affair, and the other three sides were much lower than the eventual height they would achieve in the 1960s. The pitch had a pronounced slope, running towards the pavilion and a very narrow pitch at 65 yards, which in 1931 the Scottish League ordered to be widened by at least five yards. It has since been widened further to meet UEFA criteria.

For many years Tannadice had one of the stranger quirks of Scottish football grounds, which survived into the 1980s. Half way up one of the floodlight pylons there was what appeared to be a garden shed. It held tools and fuse boxes essential for the upkeep of the lights.

■ *More than 22,000 attended the Dundee derby Scottish Cup first round replay on January 30, 1951.*

■ *The next two photos, taken at roughly 10 year intervals, show the evolution of Tannadice from roughly the same angle.*

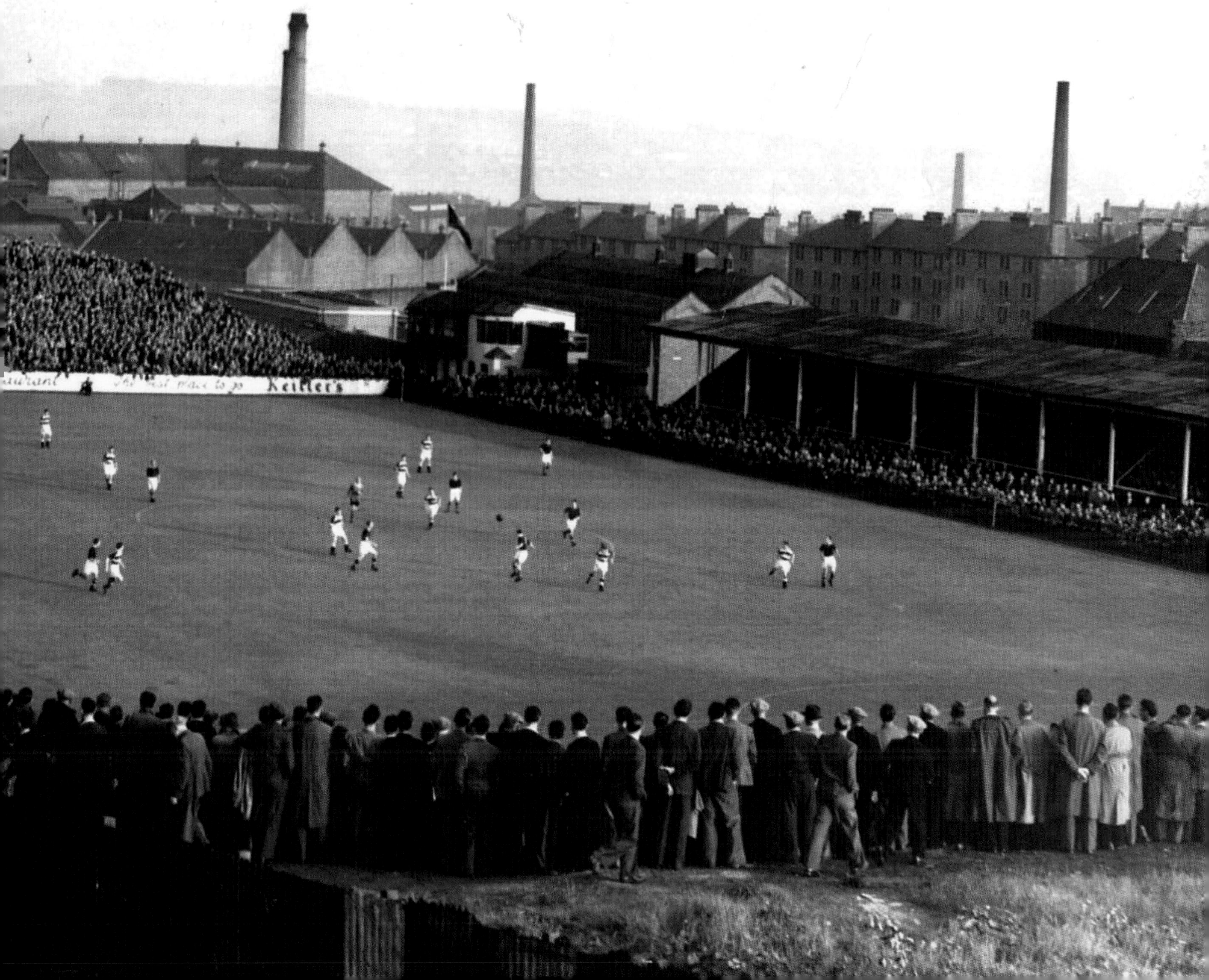
Keiller's

■ *1961 – Just before major reconstruction work begins. The Shed, however, has been given a roof.*

■ *1972 – (United v. Aberdeen on February 5).*
The new stand and steeper, higher terracing
have been created.

SMITH HOOD FUELS
Austin Morris
Clydesdale Bank
SKOL SKOL SKOL
WILDCAT jeans
SCOTWELD DISTRIBUTORS (DUNDEE)
SUPPLIERS OF ARC & GAS WELDING EQUIPMENT
739494
Grant's STANDFAST SCOTCH WHISKY

■ 1980 – The north-side terracing getting its 'Ray Stewart' roof, paid for by the full-back's transfer, for a reported £430,000 to West Ham the previous year. A large number of Scottish football clubs, especially the provincial ones, have financed their ground improvements with the transfer of players to English clubs over the decades.

TIKLAS anoraks

SCOTWELD of DUNDEE
Supply OX ACETYLENE EQUIPMENT

Telford Street & Kingsmills

Caledonian & Inverness Thistle

Caledonian, formed in 1885, were founder members of the Highland League in 1893. The club was awarded the Rothman's Football Yearbook award for 'outstanding non-league club' in 1981-82 and won the fiercely competitive Highland League no less than 18 times.

Their home ground was Telford Street Park, built in 1926 close by the Caledonian Canal.

■ *Telford Street Park in 1968 and, above, just before shutting its turnstiles for the last time.*

Thistle were also a Highland institution with a long, proud history, being winners of the very first Highland League Championship and renowned giant-killers in the Scottish Cup. Kilmarnock fans will recall a painful 3-0 reverse at the hands of the Jags in the 1984-85 campaign. Their Kingsmills ground was opened in 1895.

The two clubs, along with third Inverness powerhouse Clachnacuddin, were deadly rivals. In 1994, however, the Scottish Football League restructured to four divisions – with room for extra clubs.

Amid some chicanery and rumours of dark deeds, there were claims that the SFL might look favourably on a joint application so Caley and Thistle, despite bitter opposition among both sets of fans, became Caledonian Thistle. 'Inverness' was added two years later, at the request of Inverness District Council.

The new club played at Telford Street until 1996 when they moved to the Tulloch Caledonian Stadium, in the shadow of the Kessock Bridge over the Beauly Firth.

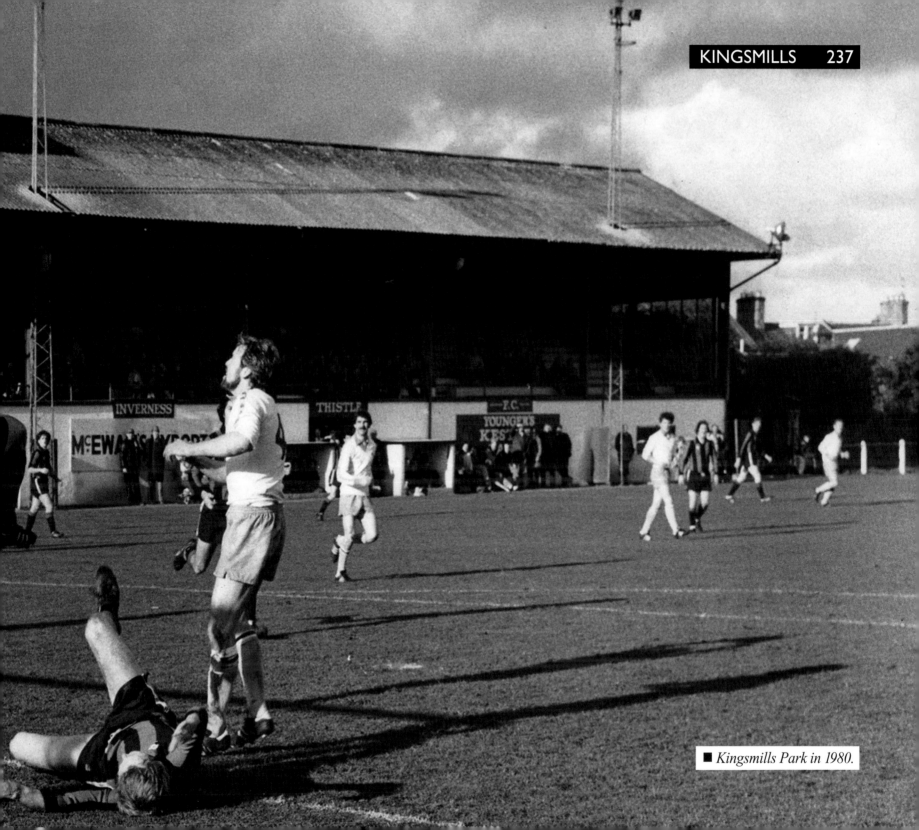

■ *Kingsmills Park in 1980.*

Tynecastle
Heart of Midlothian

■ *Tynecastle in 1959 (this picture hangs in the Hearts boardroom).*

© *Heart of Midlothian FC*

Hearts owe their existence to a dance craze. The quadrille swept Europe in the late 19th Century, it was a demanding discipline requiring energy and athleticism. Several members of the Heart of Mid-Lothian Quadrille Assembly Club attended an exhibition of association football at Raimes Park in the village of Bonnington, then on Edinburgh's periphery, in 1873 and reckoned this rough and tumble game was something they might have a go at. They bought a ball, started kicking it about and one of the giants of Scottish football was born.

Hearts were created in 1874, although the precise date isn't known. Their early home fixtures were at the East Meadows. Matches there were a problem, though. It was a busy place and spectators milling about would interfere with play. Important fixtures were played at the Edinburgh Football Association's grounds at Powburn, where they were able to charge an admission fee.

By 1879, the club was on a sound enough financial footing to secure its own park at Powderhall. The move to Dalry came in 1881 – but not to the Tynecastle of today. The original ground was a few hundred yards south, where Wardlaw Street and Place are now. The new Tynecastle was opened on land leased from Edinburgh Corporation with a friendly against Bolton Wanderers in 1886.

■ *Tynecastle in 1971.*

■ *The Gorgie Road end, backed by tenements. Legend has it that when Hearts installed a scoreboard some residents applied for reduced rates payments as their view was now restricted.*

■ *The rear of the old Main Stand.*

The Scottish Cup win in 1891 financed a new clubhouse and a roof was built on the original south stand in 1892. A small stand and pavilion were put up in 1903 and a programme of extensions to the terracing in 1906 brought capacity up to almost 62,000.

Percy Dawson was sold to Blackburn Rovers in 1914. His world record fee of £2,500 helped fund a new pitch-length main stand which would stay in place until 2017. Tynecastle's ash and wooden sleeper terraces were concreted in the mid-1950s, making it Scotland's first all-concreted ground.

The roof over the North British Distillery side and north-west corner was erected in 1959, funded by the sale of Dave McKay to Tottenham.

■ *Left: Crowd control in 1990.*

■ *Right: Using the terraces for balance training routines in 1964.*

Victoria Park

Ross County

Ross County played in the Highland League, from their founding in 1929 until they were voted in to the Scottish Leagues, alongside Caley Thistle, in time for the 1994-95 season.

They play at Victoria Park, set within Jubilee Park, in the bonny town of Dingwall, Ross & Cromarty. It is one of the few Scottish football stadiums adjacent to a caravan park.

The modern ground, re-named Global Energy Stadium in 2012, carries the distinction of having a capacity of 6,451, which is more than a thousand higher than the population of Dingwall.

The Jail End, named because the old County Jail and Sheriff Court is behind it, was terraced with money raised by receipts from the estimated 8,000-strong crowd that attended the Scottish Cup second round encounter with Rangers on February 19, 1966.

Rangers won 2-0 and would go on to lift the cup that year with a 1-0 replay win over Celtic. This was notable as the only season in Scottish football history in which Celtic and Rangers have finished first and second in all three domestic competitions.

■ *Victoria Park's wooden West Stand, which was replaced in 2012.*

© Donnie MacBean

Wee Bit Sna

The idea of a winter shutdown has been swirling about Scottish football for decades, like a never-ending blizzard. The problem is that, at times, it can be a little cold here. The harsh winters of 1947 and 1963, in particular, saw much comment on the idea of summer, not winter, football.

But sometimes the matches weren't postponed. Sometimes Scottish stadiums put on games in conditions that would horrify the modern footballer.

Groundsmen went to great lengths to make pitches playable, including the use of straw or sand strewn deeply across the pitch, or even braziers to thaw the ground.

They weren't all-weather pitches as we know them today, they were just played on in all weathers.

■ *Left: Spot-the-ball at Dens Park after a heavy snowfall in 1982.*

■ *Right: Third Lanark enlisted their first team squad in the push to get Cathkin Park playable for the visit of East Fife in February 1963. Inside-forward Sammy Baird was in charge of the pneumatic drill breaking up the ice.*

■ *Barrow-loads of sand spread on to Dundee's snow-covered Dens Park, with the crowd in place, shortly before kick-off against Ayr United in December 1937.*

"KING GEORGE IV"
WHISKY

■ *The shallow end of Dunfermline's*
East End Park in early March 1954.
The game was listed as 'in doubt'.

■ *'Och, it's fine'. A pitch inspection at Easter Road in 1960.*

■ *Rangers beat Third Lanark in a Scottish Cup third round second replay in 1954. The snow on the pitch didn't merit a mention in most newspapers' match reports.*

Hampden. 1980. Cold.

DUNDEE UN. 3, ALBION R. 0.

Half-time—0-0. Scorers—Irvine (75 min.), Gillespie (77), Howieson (85).

THE Coatbridge men provided much stiffer opposition than expected, but were well skelped in the end.

Tannadice was like the Sahara, but it was no day for sand-dancers. The lad who held on too long was liable to sit down very suddenly on a bare patch.

Those bumps must have been painful, with the pitch iron-hard under its sandy overcoat.

United proved a skilful and speedy game could be played on this surface. They moved the ball well on the ground and only bad finishing kept them from sewing things up by half-time.

■ *United officials decided the Tannadice pitch was probably a little hard a few days before that 1963 cup tie...*

Dundee United are known as 'The Arabs', although their official nickname is 'The Terrors'. The Arabian label came, legend has it, because United adapted well to a sand-covered pitch. It was common in the days before undersoil heating to spread pitches with sand when they were bone-hard, get the ref to bounce a ball on it and declare the match on. Saturday games usually attracted higher crowds than midweek games.

And so it was with United. Except there is no agreement on which game was 'the sand one'.

These two pictures are from January 21, 1963, one of the coldest winters Scotland has ever suffered.

United played Albion Rovers in a Scottish Cup first-round tie on January 26, and won 3-0 after strenuous efforts to get the pitch playable. The gate was 12,000, with takings of £1,532 (cup crowds and cash had to be published at that time).

Mystery solved then? Well, not quite.

There doesn't seem to be any record of United being called 'Arabs' at the time. Indeed, the term didn't gain widespread use until the late 1970s or early '80s. And the fans are called Arabs (not least by themselves) not the players.

■ ... so employed a team of road workers, and a heat blasting machine used for laying tarmac, to get the game on. After the navvies did their worst, several tons of sand were spread on the pitch. And the 'Arabs' name sprung from there. Possibly.

■ *The rule was, as shown at Dens Park in 1963, if the ref could see the lines he could put the game on...*

■...*Even if a snowplough was needed to get down to the lines – as seen here at Muirton in 1968.*